At the Table with the Family

Oct. 10, 2008

To Dr. Lorinsen,
With thanks and
best wishes.

At the Table with the Family

Quirico S. Samonte, Jr.

Illustrated by

Judith E. Samonte

First Page Publications
12103 Merriman • Livonia, MI 48150
1-800-343-3034 • Fax (734) 525-4420
www.firstpagepublications.com

Publisher's Cataloging-in-Publication
(Provided by Quality Books, Inc.)

Samonte, Quirico S.
At the table with the family / Quirico S. Samonte, Jr. ; illustrated by Judith E. Samonte.
p.cm.
ISBN 1-928623-41-7

1. Samonte, Quirico S. 2. Filipino Americans--Biography. 3. Educators--Michigan--Biography. 4. Immigrants--United States--Biography. 5. Family life--Philippines--History. 6. Philippines--Social conditions--History. 7. Philippines--History--Japanese occupation, 1942-1945. I. Samonte, Judith E. II. Title.

E184.F4S26 2004 977.40049921
QBI33-2052

Dedication

To Judy, Cristina, Cynthia & Brooklyn
who are custodians of a precious legacy, a part of the
tapestry of America's diverse cultures.

Acknowledgement

What wonderful memories they are! I remember fondly the many members of my extended family who helped make them possible. I am equally grateful to the relatives and friends who helped in various ways to weave the stories into a beautiful design by verifying some of my recollections, and suggesting ways to refine the narration. To be able to describe more fully their valuable contributions to this project, I have listed them under "Conversations" at the end of the book. Two other special persons who labored through the different stages of preparing the manuscript for publication should be mentioned: Sarah Hart, the Acquisitions Editor for First Page Publications, has been very helpful with her skill in coordinating the editing of the manuscript and her sensitivity to cultural diversity. Judith Samonte, my wife, provided the glue that held the whole project together through rigorous editing, analytical discussions, and adding those delightful and descriptive illustrations. She has been an indispensable co-producer of this book. I cannot thank her enough for all her contributions.

Table of Contents

Part III

Part IV

Epilogue

List of Photographs

Photographs following page 38:

Photographs following page 138:

Photographs following page 188:

Cristina and Cynthia with Grandpa Elzinga.

Fortunato Samonte (Uncle Fort) and Venancia Siazon Samonte (Aunt Ven) as early Filipino immigrants to the United states in the 1920s.

Photographs following page 254:

Coffee break for teachers at Ann Arbor Pioneer High School where I taught to "gain public school experience." 1962.

With the US Ambassador to Swaziland explaining the Mobile Teacher Center and its introduction to Swaziland. 1980.

Visiting school children in Swaziland. 1979.

Visiting school children in Swaziland. 1979.

Field trip in a village near Hodeida, North Yemen. 1984.

Field trip to the highlands of North Yemen. 1985.

Photograph on page 354:

Judith Samonte and Quirico Samonte, Jr.

List of Illustrations

Illustrations by Judith Samonte

Illustration by Brooklyn Dimitrie

Other Illustrations

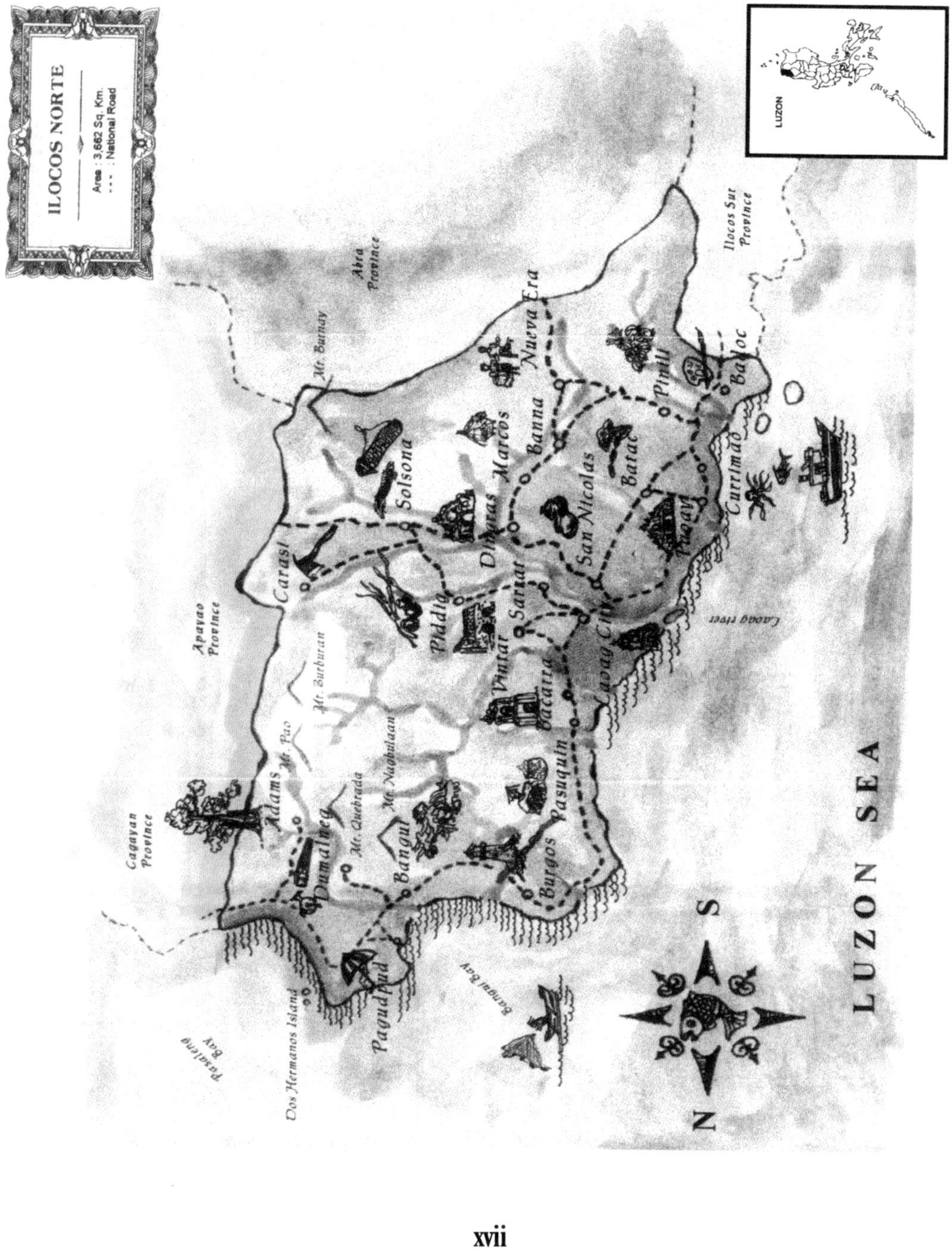
ILOCOS NORTE
Area : 3,662 Sq. Km.
- - - : National Road
LUZON
Abra Province
Ilocos Sur Province
Apayao Province
Cagayan Province
Pasaleng Bay
Dos Hermanos Island
Bangui Bay
Laoag river
Mt. Burnay
Mt. Burburan
Mt. Pao
Mt. Quebrada
Mt. Naobulaan
Pagudpud
Dumalneg
Adams
Bangui
Burgos
Pasuquin
Bacarra
Vintar
Laoag City
Piddig
Carasi
Sarrat
Dingras
Solsona
San Nicolas
Marcos
Banna
Nueva Era
Batac
Paoay
Currimao
Pinili
Badoc
N
S
LUZON SEA

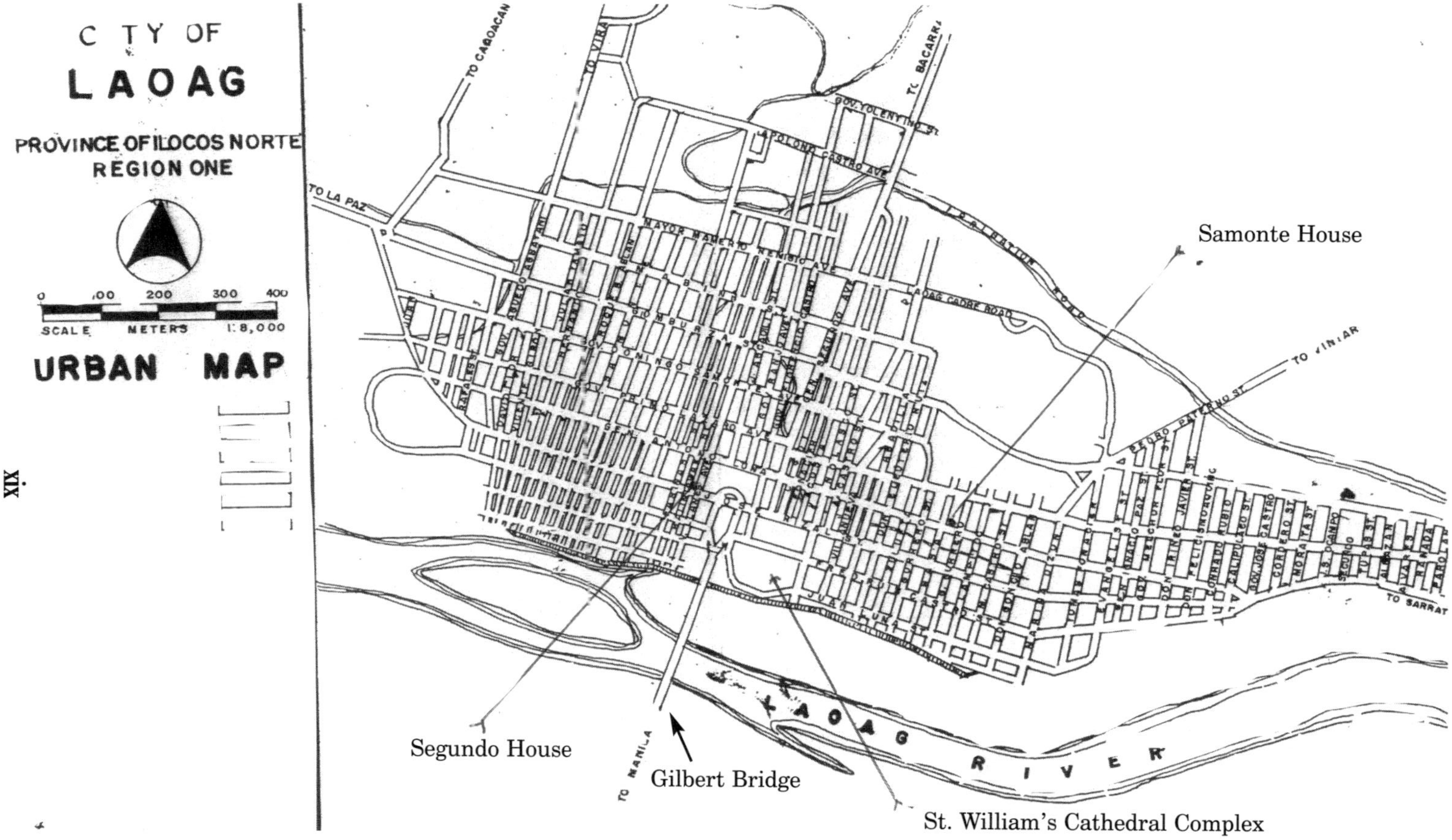
CITY OF
LAOAG
PROVINCE OF ILOCOS NORTE
REGION ONE
0 100 200 300 400
SCALE METERS 1:8,000
URBAN MAP
TO LA PAZ
TO CAGOACAN
TO VIRA
TO BACARRA
TO VINTAR
TO SARRAT
TO MANILA
MAYOR MAMERTO NEMISIO AVE
LAOAG CADRE ROAD
JUAN LUNA ST
LAOAG RIVER
Samonte House
Segundo House
Gilbert Bridge
St. William's Cathedral Complex

Abbreviated Segundo and Samonte (facing page) family tree: Showing first names and nicknames of relatives mentioned in this account and other cousins of the author, most of whom have married, have children, grandchildren and interesting stories of their own.

* Widow of Feliciano Madamba.

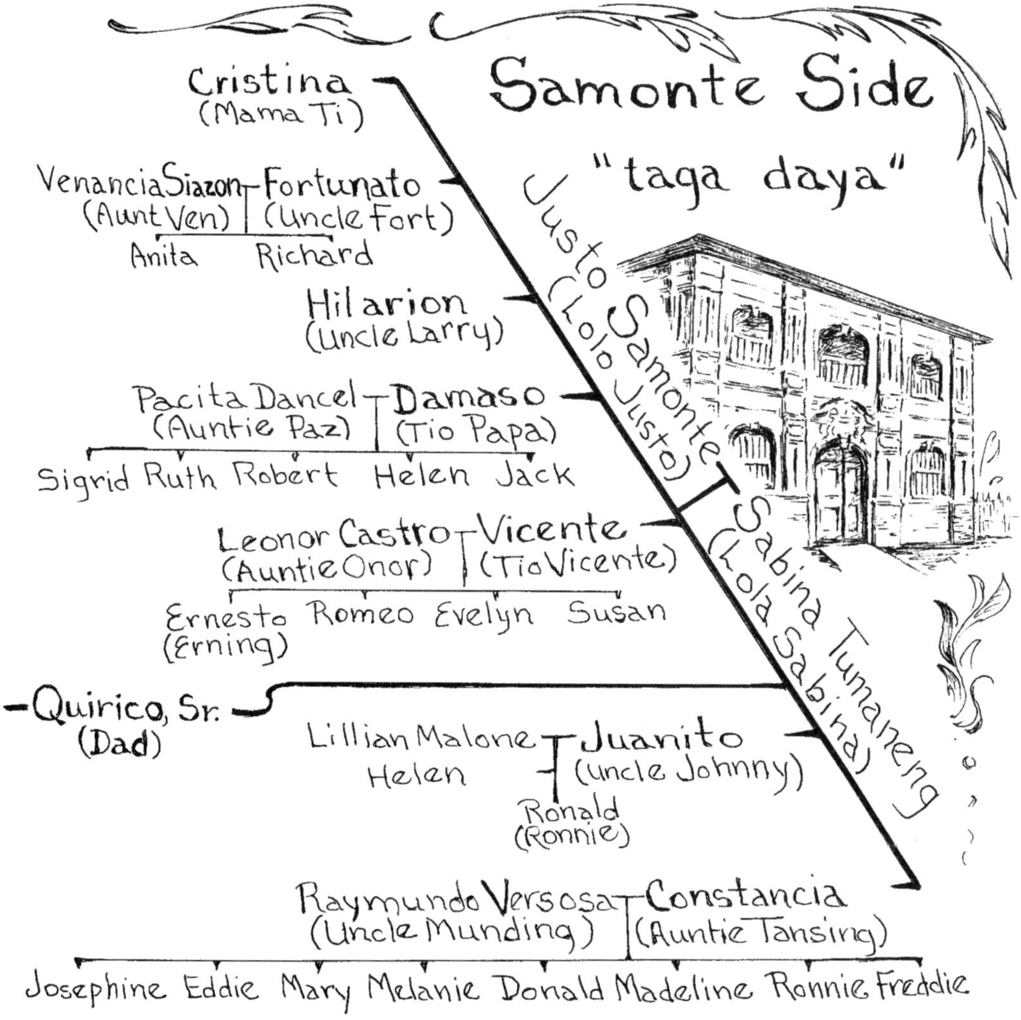

Note: The marriage of Quirico T. Samonte and Felicidad C. Segundo – as well as succeeding generations of that union are shown on the next page.

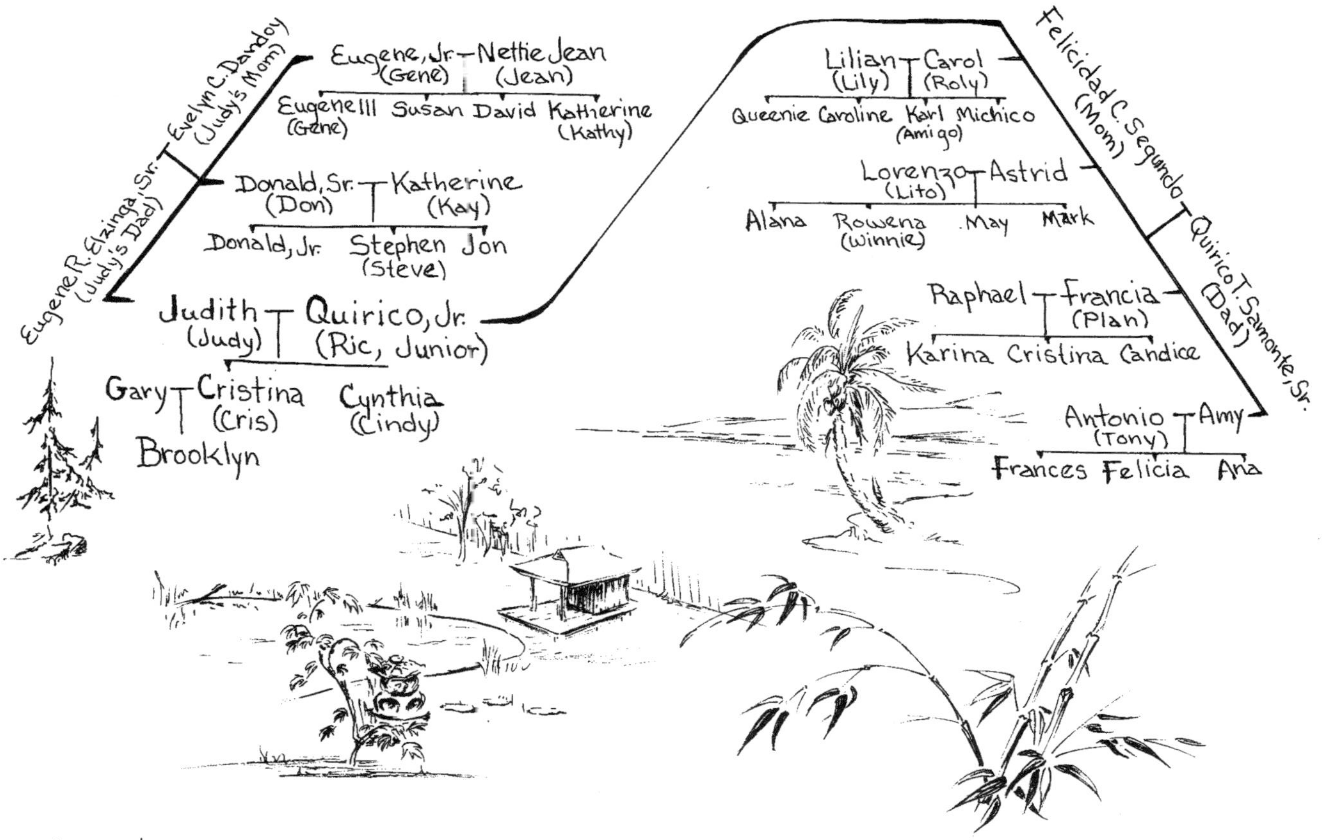

Abbreviated Elzinga and Samonte family tree from the late 1920s (continued from previous pages) - Showing first names and nicknames of relatives mentioned in this account - and other cousins of the author's children - many of whom have also now married and have children and interesting stories of their own.

Introduction

The idea of putting these recollections together was inspired by the Samonte family reunion held in Manila in November, 2001. It would have been useful if I had thought about writing them earlier so that the resulting publication could have been shared with any of those who attended the event and who may have been interested. Starting the book has, nonetheless, gained momentum and I have continued to work on it. Maybe my own family, especially my grandson, Brooklyn, will find the time and inclination to read it someday to know more about members of his family on the other side of the Pacific Ocean.

In retrospect I wish I had been more inquisitive with older members of the family while they were still living. It would have been interesting to find out what life was like when they were children, about their school and their teachers, how *Lolo* met *Lola* (terms of reference for grandfather and grandmother), and all that sort of thing.

Although these stories are intended mainly for reading by curious relatives, if there is any interest in these stories outside the family, that would be welcome too.

I should say something about the title of this book, *At the Table with the Family*. While growing up in the 1930s and 40s in the town of Laoag, the provincial capital of Ilocos Norte, noon and evening meals were occasions when we assembled as a family, including my grandparents, my mother and father, and some of Mother's unmarried siblings. Mother's newly married siblings would eventually separate from the extended family to be on their own as they gradually secured more stable employment and more adequate income. Whether I was with the Segundos, on Mother's side, or with the Samonte extended family, on Father's side, gathering at the table was a pleasant social occasion filled with entertaining stories, commentaries on what was happening in town or elsewhere, and, of course, inquiries to the children about school. When guests sometimes joined us, it made mealtime even more interesting, not to mention having additional special dishes prepared for the occasion.

Without television, radio, or an overly heavy work and social schedule, mealtime was leisurely. It was one of the most important ways through which I got to know my relatives. I learned what they believed, what choices they made and why. Serious accounting of mischievous behavior was prudently postponed to a more private session, usually with the disciplinarian of the family.

There might still be some of us who long for the days when, at the table with the family, we got to know more about each other. I do not think that spirit of family togetherness is totally extinct. It may be on the list of endangered species, but we catch sight of it once in a while, even in the United States, when we celebrate Thanksgiving or Christmas dinner. As we now go our separate ways, whether eating in front of the television or rushing somewhere for an appointment, we find it more difficult to connect with one another. Wouldn't it be nice if we could continue to observe the spirit of these special holidays everyday?

The recipes included at the end of the book are associated with some of the people mentioned in this book. They are based partly on my recollections and experiences in the United States as an immigrant from the Philippines. They are greatly simplified for convenience and economy since they are also intended for some cousins, nieces and nephews, now settled in the United States, who sometimes long for dishes that they remember from home. The recipes have also been adjusted for homesick relatives who have now become conscious about weight, shape and physical fitness.

Some of the words in the book are Ilocano terms used in Laoag, Ilocos Norte, including those that are obviously of Spanish and English derivations. These are italicized in the text. Please refer to the Glossary towards the end of the book for translations.

Part I

I Remember

Like the proverbial view from a mountain top where one might see an inspiring, panoramic landscape, I like to believe that the legacy from my elders is a picture that is equally uplifting. This little volume is an autobiography, but I have included stories about some of my elders and a few others who have influenced me in one way or another. I remember them in various ways: they provided clarity when things were not clear to me, humor and levity when I was sad, encouragement and inspiration to persevere when giving up would have been an easier, but cowardly, option, and other happy and funny memories which I have treasured all these years. In narrating these stories, I hope I can contribute to preserving part of their legacy. For succeeding generations, it is a good idea to be in touch with their past as they look forward to the future. It is exciting to contemplate what lies ahead with incredible innovations in technology, new opportunities for employment, diverse life-styles, expanded horizons for travel, greater possibilities for good health and longer life. The possibilities of a better life materially are indeed exciting.

On the other hand, I believe the challenge of achieving a more meaningful, harmonious and compassionate life for individuals and for society seems to be more complicated and elusive than ever. One needs only to look at the increase in broken homes, crime, juvenile delinquency, kidnappings, wars, and allegations of increasing corruption in the public and private sectors. In this context, I like to believe that values like honor, courage, perseverance and compassion are still relevant today. Confronted by rapid technological changes, the growing influence of popular culture, the pressure to conform to corporate expectations and the inclination to be politically correct, traditional values might help provide an individual with an inner compass and gyroscope for direction and balance. To be sure, life was not always sweetness and light for our elders, but how they confronted their challenges could provide insights for us to consider.

I have a relatively large extended family, and there are other relatives who have also influenced me but are mentioned only briefly in this book. Because of my limited face-to-face contact with some of them, or no contact at all in some cases as a result of separation by geography, I did not have sufficient first-hand experience with them to feel confident writing as extensively about them as I have with those included in this book. They attracted my attention, nonetheless, since the immediate members of my family talked about these geographically distant relatives whenever there was news written in the newspapers or mentioned on the radio about them, such as their promotions or new work assignments.

Thus, some of my accomplished "absent" relatives were also role models as I learned about them through talks at the table with the family. On my mother's side, for example, was her cousin, General Fidel Segundo, who was one of the first Filipinos sent to West Point. He returned to the Philippines to pursue a distinguished career in the Philippine Armed Forces. On my father's side there were a number of cousins who were recognized for their role in public life in the Philippines after returning from their studies abroad. There was Dr. Domingo Samonte who earned his medical degree from the University of Iowa. He returned to the Philippines to serve his country in various capacities. He was elected governor of the province of Ilocos Norte and, later, served in the national government under President Quezon. There was Dr. Vedasto Samonte, brother of Domingo, who earned his Ph.D. in political science from the University of Iowa. After his return to the Philippines, he joined the University of the Philippines as a member of the faculty and, later, as an administrator of the university. There is General Ernesto Samonte Mata who was a graduate of the Philippine Military Academy, and other army officer's schools in the United States. He returned to the Philippines to distinguish himself as a guerrilla leader during the Japanese occupation and, later, became Chief of Staff of the Philippine Armed Forces and Secretary of Defense.

Closer to home, there is *Tia* Cely (Araceli Barba Segundo) who is the widow of *Tio* Bening, a brother of Mother. *Tia* Cely was my private piano teacher when I was in elementary school. I thought she was very expressive as a musician. I was equally impressed by her refined nature, and how soft-spoken she was even when asking whether I remembered to practice the piano exercises at home when obviously I had not! I continue to be impressed by those fine qualities of her character to this day.

Thus, even if my contact with these relatives was limited, they influenced me positively for I found what I learned about them inspiring indeed.

Mom

Upon entering the "Big Church," the popular name of St. William's Cathedral in Laoag, which was constructed by the Spaniards during the second half of the seventeenth century, one comes upon two marble fonts containing holy water. People dipped a finger into one of these and made the sign of the cross. Mindful of what the adults did, I tried to imitate them when I went to church with Mother. When Mother dipped a finger into the font, she apparently kept an eagle eye on me while she quickly made the sign of the cross. I stood on my toes so I could reach over with the idea of doing the same, and a quick warning came from her before I could touch the water. "Germs," she said, audible enough for me to hear. That was a code word she had taught me before I was three or four years old when she wanted me to refrain from doing something that related to hygiene or sanitation. Very quickly I withdrew my hand and followed her quietly as we looked

With Mother at St. William's Cathedral in Laoag

for a place to sit. I guess this was typical of Mother; she was good about observing the usual social conventions but always protective of her family.

It is probably fair to say that Mother came from a family that the people in Laoag would have considered then as "prominent." They were landowners, and my maternal grandfather, *Lolo* Nicolas Segundo, was one of the early and successful lawyers in town. *Lolo* Nicolas and *Lola* Leoncia were fluent in Spanish, having graduated from schools where Spanish was the language of instruction.

Lola Leoncia liked to entertain with lavish dinners whenever there were visiting dignitaries in town, and on special occasions like birthdays. I knew when some special visitors were coming—the signs were unmistakable. Some of the farm tenants would come to town to help tidy up the yard, and there would be extra cooks at the house, including the indispensable *Lakay* Chitong and *Lakay* Gorio, the popular "chefs" of the town. The finishing touch to all these preparations was bringing out the huge *alfombra* (carpet) for the living room after the hardwood floor had been polished. Polishing the wood floor was accomplished using the usual combination of coconut husk for scrubbing and melted candle for waxing. Then the final buffing was done with a large piece of cloth which I sometimes sat on to provide additional weight as the houseboy pulled it around. Whatever political and social agenda my grandparents had with all this entertaining, I left up to them. I occupied myself with my own priorities: I made sure I had my generous portions of the desserts and sweets like *leche flan* and *santol* preserve which *Lola* Leoncia personally prepared for such events.

The folks in the western part of the town where Mother lived tended to look down in a somewhat joking manner on people who lived either in the eastern (*taga daya*) part of the town or in the extreme west "near the cemetery" (*asideg diay camposanto*). Residents "from the west" (*taga laod*) near the town plaza tended to regard themselves as better positioned in the social pecking order, provided they were not squatters. Thus, some of the geographical locations in town had significance in terms of one's ranking in the social structure. In this connection, it is noted by Alicia M.L.Coseteng in her informative and interesting book, *Spanish Churches in the Philippines*, (1972), that as the population grew and urbanization developed during the Spanish period, the church, convent, and government buildings became the religious and political center of the town. People of wealth and those who considered themselves important tended to locate their houses close to the town center or plaza. (Coseteng, 17) Perhaps this partly explains the social attitude of those like my mother's family who resided close to the town plaza. Given this perspective, it was confusing to my young mind that while I qualified as *taga laod* because Mother was from that section of town, Father was *taga daya*, from the eastern part of the town and what that implied socially. It is not surprising that Mom and Dad decided to elope when they were still high school students. Mom added that *Tio* Deriong, her oldest brother, gave chase as a matter of obligation but did not try too hard since he was also a friend of my father! They were married on March 27, 1927. From this union, I was born half *taga daya* and half *taga laod*, a bit confusing to a growing boy in terms of who I was socially and where my loyalties should be.

In spite of her upper-class background relative to the social structure of Laoag, Mother impressed me as a person of humility. Equally memorable was her no-nonsense and pragmatic approach to life: she was hard-working, a skillful bargainer and resourceful in making ends meet when she and Father were working to raise a young family. Between the two of them, I tended to think of Mom as a realist while Dad was more of an idealist. Together they worked well as a team.

Shopping at bargain stores located in the Central Market or in Divisoria in Manila was special and fun for Mother, especially if she found some *retazos* (remnants) of sewing material that fitted into some design she might have had in mind. It was amazing how she could look at a picture of a dress in an old Sears & Roebuck or Montgomery Wards catalog and reproduce it without the benefit of a store-bought pattern. Pajamas, robes, shirts, and dresses for the family were produced from her old Singer treadle sewing machine. When I was in grade school she made shirts for me. As I grew older I thought it would be nice to have a store-bought shirt with labels inside the collar like those worn by some of the other kids in school. She took care of that quickly. For those that she made for me, she took labels from Dad's old shirts and sewed them into my new shirts! I could never adjust completely, however, to her practice of buying me shoes that were usually two sizes too big because, according to her, I would "soon grow into them." So whenever I had a new pair, she usually stuck wads of cotton inside the front part of the shoes to make them "fit."

Another event stands out in my mind regarding Mother's resourcefulness. The Segundo house was right next to the only movie house in town, Cine Reyes. It was a warehouse-type building; the roof and walls were made of galvanized iron, and it had wooden benches where the joints were infested with *kiteb* (bedbugs). Because of the bedbugs, the movie house was popularly known as "*Cine Kiteb.*" Seating arrangements were divided into three groups: five to ten *centavos* for the *Entrada General*, fifteen *centavos* for the *Butaca* situated behind *Entrada General*, and twenty *centavos* for the *Palco* which was the balcony above the *Butaca*. Children that measured below a marker etched on the frame of the wooden door paid half. The seating arrangements tended to separate different social classes, but the bedbugs were more egalitarian and did not pay much attention to social status. All the seats were equally infested with bedbugs no matter what you paid!

One evening Uncle Damaso and Auntie Paz decided to go to the movie. They had Sigrid with them, their eldest daughter who was then an infant and nursing. They stopped at the Segundo house where Auntie Paz changed into a different dress, and left Sigrid with my mother. Mother, who was then nursing my brother, Roly, baby-sat for Sigrid. Halfway through the movie, Sigrid started crying. The usual procedure of checking the diaper and offering milk through breast-feeding followed. Sigrid refused Mother's milk and continued to cry with even greater vigor.

Father and Mother talked about sending the houseboy to the movie house to get Auntie Paz. They decided not to when Mother came up with an idea. She wondered if Sigrid could tell the difference between Mother and Auntie Paz on the basis of smell. Based on this speculation, Mother decided to put on the clothes that Auntie Paz had left at the house when she changed into a different dress to go to the movies. Mother tried again to breast-feed Sigrid in the darkened room. Sure enough, Sigrid went for Mother's milk with *gusto*! Could it be that Sigrid was just hungry and did not care who was breast-feeding her, or did Mother's changing into Auntie Paz's dress make the difference? Whatever it was, I was impressed by Mother's ability, as she did in other situations, to search for practical solutions and make use of materials that were on hand.

Mother would not miss an opportunity, it seemed to me, to collect good information she thought might be useful to her even from street vendors. Barefoot vendors, selling various items like firewood, fresh or cooked fish, vegetables, or live chickens, passed by the house on their way to the public market. The men carried two loads of firewood or other things with a pole on their shoulders. Each bundle was suspended at opposite ends of a slightly pliable bamboo that flexed mildly with the gait of the carrier. More eye-catching were the women who balanced one or two baskets on their heads without holding them as they walked smartly toward the market. Once in a while Mother would hail a vendor over to the house. She sometimes commented on how well the women from the fishing villages (west of the town along the shore of the China Sea) prepared steamed fish that were still firm but moist with the flavor of vinegar and ginger. One time she complimented her favorite vendor about the quality of her cooking, and asked if she would share the secret with Mother. The woman, obviously pleased, advised not putting any water in the pan, because the vinegar and moisture from the flesh of the fish would be sufficient to steam over slow heat.

One thing I remember about Mother and her brothers and sisters was their buoyant sense of humor. In contrast, Father's brothers and sisters were more serious; their humor was more restrained. This difference between the two families is reflected in Cousin Ruth's (Samonte-Limjuco) account of one of her visits home. Ruth was then with the Department of Foreign Affairs of the Philippines. With the rank of Ambassador, she served as Deputy Permanent Representative to the United Nations. She wrote to me on November 29, 2001:

> When I was home on assignment in the late 80's, I would visit with Auntie Eling and Uncle Quirico quite often. We used to spend hours chatting. Meal times would stretch into hours. Uncle Quirico (Father) would discourse endlessly on politics and the foibles and fancies of politicians. Auntie Eling (Mother) would regale me with stories and recollections of the past, delivered with such aplomb and humor that we would burst out into gales of laughter.

Auntie Alice, the wife of Mother's brother, Miguel (*Tio* Gli), added her recollections about Mother in her letter to me dated October 16, 2002. She wrote:

> I wish to add something more about how thoughtful and resourceful I thought she was. I recall an experience I had about shopping in downtown Manila with *Manang* Anching (sister of Mother) and Manang Eling (Mother). In Villalobos was a set of table appointments—dishes, spoons and forks, etc.—that struck my fancy. Since I had not prepared my budget for such a purchase, I was in no position to buy them. I could only imagine how nice they would have looked on my table, and that was all I could do. Two weeks later, in one of the packages

> from my brother Paquito, also a friend of *Manang* Anching and *Manang* Eling, was a letter from your mom informing me that there had been a 'fire sale' at Villalobos and the set I wanted was on sale at practically a give-away price. She remembered how much I wanted the set and she bought them for me which I paid for later at a very affordable price indeed. It was for me, a remote dream come true. Again, her thoughtfulness, resourcefulness and frugality came through, and these are just examples of some of the fine qualities I remember about her.

During one of my visits to the Philippines after Mother was gone, I stayed at the house in Project 6, Quezon City, where my sister Amy, her husband Tony, and their three little girls now live. While waiting for lunch, I rested in the garden in Father's favorite *butaca* (reclining chair). I overheard the chatter and laughter coming from the kitchen as the maids prepared lunch. Nothing unusual except my ears perked up when I heard this laughter from one of Amy's daughters which sounded very much like Mother! With amusement, I listened more closely at the striking similarity between Mother's laughter, that of my niece, and my own daughter Cristina's hearty laughter. I guess we like to believe that our loved ones are not gone forever. They are with us in many ways—in things we believe and value, in cherished memories, and sometimes we see a little bit of them in our children and grandchildren.

The role and responsibilities assumed by Mother were probably typical for the period, for the location, for her education, and for her social class. We did not have labor-saving devices that are now taken for granted in a middle-class American family. We did not, for example, have a motorized lawn mower, washing machine, clothes dryer, floor polisher or a vacuum cleaner. Instead, we had one or two live-in houseboys who did the gardening, heavy house cleaning, and ran errands. In addition, we had two or three live-in maids who, under Mother's careful training and supervision, did light house cleaning, laundry and ironing, cooking and also looked after the small children. Our relationships with the houseboys and maids may be characterized as paternalistic. Any of them who showed promise as a student would be encouraged to go school, and even to college at our family's expense. Medical care was provided for them when needed. Because of this bond, a houseboy or maid might even choose to stay with us for life, and a few of them have actually done so for our extended family.

Perhaps these arrangements with the helpers would not meet the approval of activists and advocates of laborers' rights from the industrialized world who visit countries like the Philippines. In their role as self-appointed reformers, they might disapprove of such use of household help, if they fail to appreciate the interplay of low-level technology, the absence of workable institutionalized protection for laborers and children, low literacy levels which result in limited options for employment, a rapidly expanding poor population, and a government administration that is frequently riddled with corruption. This corruption is compounded by foreign governments that donate aid and support corrupt officials, so that these donor governments can get what they want, such as military bases or concessions for natural resources or commercial development.

Consequently, trying to reform such household arrangements could be a disappointing experience for well-intentioned foreign volunteers who are inspired to venture to developing countries.

For example, there was the case of a Peace Corps volunteer from a small town in the Upper Peninsula of Michigan, who announced presumptuously in the local newspaper that he selected the Philippines for his Peace Corps assignment to "help in the social development of the Filipinos!" It could also be frustrating for someone like the misguided official of the United States State Department, a cultural attaché, who proclaimed at my group orientation in an African country that we were there "to bring culture to these people!" Whatever or whoever the catalyst for an activist might be, it does not, unfortunately, alter the dynamics of slow and painful change in developing countries.

This analysis should not be taken, however, as an endorsement of the social system that influenced the role Mother had as a housewife and homemaker. While I recognize there is always room for improvement, I also realize that it was not, relative to that period, repressive. There were opportunities for girls to be educated as prescribed by law, and those who completed a college degree were encouraged to seek employment where it was available. As a matter of fact, the Philippines is one of the few countries where a woman has served as the President of the country, not once, but twice.

The women of the younger generation (i.e. those born after the Second World War) in our extended family do have a different life-style as housewives compared to that during

Mother's time. Some of them have earned college degrees and some are employed in the private and public sectors. Many got married at a later age, and have fewer children. It should be noted, however, that with this younger group, there are more legal separations (divorce is not legal in the Philippines) than in Mother and Father's generation. Maybe this represents change for greater emancipation of women. Only time will tell what additional changes these developments will bring to the traditional Filipino family.

Mom was born on November 23, 1910. She passed away on October 17, 1993.

Dad

The invasion of the Philippines by Japan in December, 1941, was unexpected, swift and frightening. Just as the attack on Pearl Harbor was a surprise to the Americans in the United States, the Philippine and American armed forces in the Philippines were apparently unaware of a Japanese convoy sailing towards the Philippines, and planes based in Formosa flying towards Luzon for a bombing mission on December 8, 1941 (Dec. 7th in Hawaii). At least that was the conclusion of a Japanese officer, Capt. Tameichi Hara, when he examined American documents after the war to write his book, *Japanese Destroyer Captain*, Ballantine Books, 1961. It was not long before the roads leading away from the towns and cities throughout the Philippines were inundated with bull carts, horse-drawn *calesas*, bicycles, some buses (while gasoline lasted), and people on foot carrying an assortment of bundles as they hurriedly sought refuge in the countryside.

Landowners were fortunate to have their own farms where they could go. Those who did not have farmland either stayed in town or joined the exodus with the hope of being provided safe haven by kind landowners.

The predicament of Chinese store owners in Laoag was even more complicated. They tended to live in a cluster in the central business district; Philippine law prohibited them from owning farm property. Living in close proximity to each other also provided a greater sense of security for them. But this had the effect of isolating the Chinese socially from the rest of the community, except for those few who married into Filipino families. Remaining in town during the Japanese invasion was probably not an attractive option for the Chinese. The Sino-Japanese war, which had been going on for some time in China, made them fearful of the impending arrival of Japanese soldiers. Eventually the Chinese stores were hurriedly abandoned and became the target of extensive looting by Filipinos. This problem of looting in Laoag was effectively dealt with when two looters were shot dead on the spot by Japanese soldiers.

The Japanese couple that ran the only Japanese store in Laoag fared differently, as expected under the circumstances. That "Japanese Bazar" was operated by an elderly couple referred to as Mr. and Mrs. Kamikawa, and there were five to seven young Japanese men who worked for them as salesmen. It is interesting to note that when the Japanese occupation force finally arrived in Laoag, two of the former salesmen in Kamikawa's store put on their Japanese military uniforms, including their sabers! I remember their faces well. I frequented the Japanese Bazaar as a schoolboy because of the array of toys they had on display. When I was a bootblack, some of the salesmen were among my favorite customers. The store also served as a sanctuary of sorts when, as bootblacks, we would tease some of the Chinese vendors who would eventually chase us. We would run to the Japanese store where we knew we would be safe. The Chinese did not dare follow us.

The evacuation of my extended family from Laoag had its share of complications. Along with my cousins Erning and Romeo, I followed Auntie Cristina to the Samonte farm in Capacacan, a village of the town of Banna in the southeastern part of Ilocos Norte. Mother, Astrid and Francy fled with the Segundo family. Father and Brother Roly were stranded in Manila. Since evacuation was a hasty and confused affair, I did not know until later where Father, Mother, Roly, Astrid and Francy were.

My younger brother, Roly, recounted how in December, 1941, just after the outbreak of the war, Father traveled with him from Manila to Laoag. Roly was eight years old. Because public transportation was disrupted immediately after the Japanese occupation, travel between provinces was definitely an inconvenient and dangerous undertaking. Travel by bus from Manila to Laoag ordinarily took ten hours. It was a five-day journey for Father and Roly. They traveled during the day, sometimes on foot, sometimes by horse-drawn *calesa*. Father would carry Roly on his back when the walking got too tiresome for Roly. They also walked through rice fields to avoid Japanese checkpoints on the main road. At night they stayed at the homes of people they did not know. But residents along the way gladly offered Father and Roly shelter and safety, as they did with other travelers. During the war we learned quickly to help one another in the face of a common enemy, and that is how it was among most Filipinos during the Japanese occupation of the Philippines. Traveling at night at that early stage of the war in the Philippines would have meant risking possible encounter with a Japanese patrol, marauding bandits, or some edgy and trigger-happy *guerrilleros*. To those good people who provided safe haven, food and occasional transportation to Father and Roly in their long travel from Manila to Laoag, I am profoundly grateful.

Having the whole family together again was, needless to say, a happy event. We knew other families during the war who were less fortunate. Roly is the even-tempered and refined brother he has always been. I sometimes wish I had spent more time with him when we were younger, showing him, for example, how to make a kite, a top, a popgun or a sling shot. On second thought, maybe it is just as well that Roly spent more time with boys in his age group for I usually got other kids into all kinds of mischief anyway. Astrid is my quiet and scholarly younger sister. She could always be counted on to research problems that the family encountered now and then. Francy is my lively and multi-talented sister. She has amazed me with her skills: she quickly learned the Japanese language, she plays beautiful chords on the piano (which I have never been able to duplicate), and she excels at portrait painting, something that she has recently taken up again with dedication and energy. Amy, my youngest sister, was only six months old when I left for the United States in 1954. She reminds me of our paternal grandmother's proud and dignified bearing.

A brief explanation of why the members of my family were not together at the outbreak of the war might be in order. Because Father got married before he finished college, he worked at various jobs to support his family. Fortunately, he did quite well in the civil service examinations, and with a couple of years in college as an architecture student (Mapua Institute of Technology), he was able to find work with the government. Before the war, he worked with the Bureau of Public Works at the Laoag office. Later, he decided he should work on the completion of his college degree, so he moved to Manila. There, he found a job with the Bureau of Commerce. He worked during the day and went to college classes in the evening. He rented an apartment on Zurbaran St., Santa Cruz, Manila, across the street from a private College of Pharmacy. Mother, Roly, Astrid and I would visit during summer vacation. During the school year, eight-year-old Roly and some of my older cousins who were going to college, stayed with Father in Manila. In 1941, when Mother was expecting her fourth child, she decided she should have the baby in Laoag where she could get more help from her extended family. Francy was born in Laoag in October, 1941. These were the circumstances that led to our family's dispersal when it was time to evacuate to the farm at the outbreak of the war in the Philippines.

When Father and Roly finally rejoined the family, they stayed for a while at the Segundo farm in Surrate, Dingras. The farm was close to the base of the Cordillera Mountains. It could be reached from the town of Dingras by bull cart, horse, or walking on a dry river bed for two to three hours. A four-wheel drive vehicle could have made it easily, but there was no such thing during that time. It was a relatively well-hidden place and it was a good place for family rural refuge. Unfortunately, a guerrilla unit also thought it was a good location for one of their headquarters! Thus the members of a guerrilla unit later stayed at the Segundo farm, housed among the different nipa huts of our tenant farmers who shared their little dwellings.

Father thought it would probably be safer for the family to move to another location because the Japanese army was aggressively pursuing a "mopping-up" operation throughout the province. The guerrillas were ill-equipped and poorly organized, so there was no effective resistance against the Japanese army. The guerrillas could only ambush and run. Civilians caught in the middle paid the price, either with their lives or by being tortured by the Japanese soldiers to extract information about the guerrillas.

Moving from one place to another was one way in which evacuees insured some degree of safety. So, Father and Mother decided to move from the Segundo farm to the farm of some friends in Katebbegan, Solsona. We stayed there briefly until we felt it was safe enough to move to town in Solsona. There was a Japanese garrison in Solsona, but that did not keep some families from returning to their homes to resume some kind of normalcy in their lives.

Solsona was, before the war, a small town situated in the eastern part of Ilocos Norte. It had a short main street lined with a few trees like *camito*, *algarobo* and *damortis*, a retail store owned by a Chinese family, a public market and the usual *tiangi* or *sari sari* stores. At the end of the main street was a public square where the Roman Catholic Church and the municipal building were located. Solsona had some elementary schools (grades 1–6) in the *poblacion* as well as in some of the *barrios*, but no high school (grades 7–10). High school students transferred to Laoag where the only public provincial high school was located.

Although the town of Solsona was quite small compared to Laoag, the generosity and kindness of the people there stand out in my mind. They shared what small things they had with evacuees like us. Because the people invited us into their homes and welcomed us with warmth and friendship, Mother and Father took active part in various community activities. To minimize the anxieties of war, people had birthday parties, enjoyed occasional picnics by the Karinkin River, celebrated religious holidays (including the town fiesta), and held small family dances. Music was provided by Cosme, a blind but able violinist who was accompanied on the guitar by his son. With his wonderful rendition of music popular during those days, songs like *Maria Elena, Dolores, South of the Border, Let Me Call You Sweetheart, When You Hair Turns to Silver, Spring Time in the Rockies, Ramona,* etc., Cosme gave us comfort, enjoyment and temporary relief from the ugliness of war. I can never thank the wonderful people of Solsona enough for their kindness and friendship to my family during the war.

The Filipino families that moved into towns, whether it was in Solsona or other towns of Ilocos Norte, had to put up with the requirements of living directly under a Japanese garrison. For instance, school age children attended the public schools, which were re-opened with a pro-Japanese curriculum. This included teaching the Japanese language and the removal of any reference to the United States, except as an exploitative colonial power. Young people were expected to wake up by sunrise and assemble in designated streets to participate in exercises prescribed by the Japanese. People were required to dispose of their garbage properly instead of tossing it over the fence into the street. Drivers of horse-drawn *calesas* were told to suspend some kind of a "manure catcher" behind the horse to avoid littering the streets. There seemed to be more social discipline, which took precedence over our usual easygoing Filipino style of life. However, I did not like the policy that required Filipinos to bow to a Japanese sentry whenever we passed in front of one. Passengers in a *calesa*, for example, were expected to get out of the horse-drawn cart, line up in front of the sentry and bow in unison.

I recall an incident in Laoag when I was riding my bike with a block of ice which my family had asked me to purchase from the icehouse. I came upon a sentry and I did not bother to stop, get off my bike or bow to him. He hollered in Japanese, and from the tone of his voice, I knew he was angry. I got off my bike and apprehensively approached the sentry who was shouting at me. He gestured for me to stand next to another Filipino under the sun (*naipalag*) in the town plaza. This was a form of punishment. I must have stood there for at least four hours under a blistering tropical sun. My block of ice was completely melted by then. I had only a wet sack to show for it. *Tio* Gli, Mother's brother, commented I looked red like a cooked shrimp when I got home!

Meanwhile in Solsona, it became untenable for the Japanese to maintain a garrison and they finally abandoned the town. In turn, the guerrillas occupied the town, but they needed to maintain their vigilance since the Japanese could easily come back if they wanted to, and in fact they did make a few surprise visits. The guerrillas organized a civilian force of *bolo* men who provided all sorts of assistance such as guard duty in various locations, carriers of supplies, and fighters, if necessary, with the only weapons they had: *bolo* (knife with a large blade used as farm tool or weapon) and pointed bamboos. Father was designated as the commander for that *bolo* unit in Solsona, which numbered about five hundred men.

It should be noted that before the United States Armed Forces finally arrived in Ilocos Norte in 1945, there were different groups that claimed to be the "legitimate" guerrillas. An earlier unit was recognized and assisted by the local people, and this consisted of Filipino soldiers and volunteers who refused to surrender to the Japanese. A second group, which showed up in Ilocos Norte later on, consisted of a self-styled band whose members came mostly from outside Ilocos Norte, and they were notorious for plundering and committing atrocities in the countryside. When this latter group occupied a town or village, there was not much the people could do but serve and provide food for them. After a process of trying to eliminate each other, these two guerrilla groups finally merged. The outsiders and self-styled guerrillas gained dominance since they were able to intercept the newer arms brought in by an American submarine as well as air-drops from C–47 cargo planes. The members of the guerrillas who were accused of committing atrocities, mainly the outsiders, were eventually granted amnesty by the national government as soon as civilian authority was re-established in the Philippines after World War II.

My brother Roly recalled in an unpublished manuscript how a band of guerrillas, the outsiders, appeared in Solsona soon after the Japanese soldiers left the town. He writes:

> *"Adda dan!"* ("They are here!"), the people shouted jubilantly. As soon as Cosme, the blind musician, heard the ecstatic roar from the welcoming crowd, he started his small group of musicians. The music played and the people anxiously waited as the guerrillas approached the town. I joined the crowd and watched with excitement. As the men came into view, they looked unkempt and heavily armed with the new weapons such as Thompson's submachine guns, Carbines, Garands, and pistols that were brought by American submarines and some that were dropped from the air by cargo planes. The elation turned to terror as the town officials and the people assembled realized that the armed men turned out to be the much-feared and ruthless self-styled guerrillas, the *Pilpilmes* ("the real ones"). The tense

atmosphere was minimized somehow by the orchestra which continued playing the Philippine National Anthem, some Sousa marches, and some popular tunes like "God Bless America." What was initially a tense situation turned into a forced but festive occasion. The celebration, if we can call it that, lasted all night, and ended peacefully in the early daylight hours. The *Pilpilmes* were apparently impressed by the festivities, thus, there were no tortures or executions as the people had originally feared. But the people of Solsona continued to be apprehensive.

The following day, town officials, Dad, and *Tio* Salio were summoned to the *Pilpilmes'* camp, somewhere north of Solsona, probably in the town of Piddig. Keep in mind that the people of Solsona were very supportive of the first group of guerrillas, and Dad was the commander of the *Bolo* Battalion that the first and legitimate guerrillas had organized in Solsona. Being "invited" for questioning was not a good sign, and it terrified Mom. That night prior to Dad's departure along with the others, I overheard Mom crying. I could not sleep because I knew that Dad was probably in grave danger. At dawn Dad prepared to leave. Mom continued to dissuade him, but he assured her that it was probably better for them to go. While Astrid and Francy, my sisters, were asleep, I sat in the *sala* alone and fearful of what might happen to Dad. As he went down the stairs, I was overcome by fear with the prospect of losing Dad. I cried and screamed at the top of my voice. Dad came back, hugged me, and told me with firmness, "Don't worry. I'll be back. Be good." Then he left. It was with good reason that Mom dreaded what might happen to Dad and *Tio* Salio. Only a couple of months before the *Pilpilmes* showed up in Solsona, they surprised and massacred members of a guerrilla unit that were based in a village west of Laoag. Many of the victims were contemporaries and friends of Mom and Dad. One was Fermin Bueno, a professional Philippine Army officer who was a neighbor and boyhood friend of Father. Another was Clemente Juan, who was the driver and bodyguard of Uncle Damaso before the war. There were other victims our family knew personally. It seemed like a long time without any news from Dad or *Tio* Salio. But the next day, Dad, *Tio* Salio and the rest of the town officials who were summoned returned unharmed. They were questioned mainly about the organization of the *Bolo* Battalion of Solsona by the previous guerrilla group. A unanimous response by Dad's group that the *Bolo* Battalion was organized mainly for the protection of the people of Solsona and that they could help the *Pilpilmes* as well evidently saved their lives. And thanks also to Cosme's band, which made the *Pilpilmes*' arrival in Solsona a festive one, although it was never intended that way!

When the Japanese left Solsona and the *Pilpilmes* moved into town, some families returned to the countryside for fear of being caught in the middle, in case of a fight between the Japanese and the guerrillas. Only the inexperienced and untrained *bolo* men stayed to guard the town. One night, because of a breakdown in security on the part of the guerrillas, the Japanese soldiers came back to Solsona and surprised the *bolo* men. As a Japanese patrol approached the house where my family had lived in Solsona, Father and the houseboy, Ciriaco, then the only occupants of the house, jumped out of the back window of the one-story structure. They crept towards the creek in the back, and managed to elude the patrol.

Ciriaco stayed with us throughout the war and beyond until he passed away. He remained with us through many hardships, and was always upbeat when he talked about how much better our lives would be when the war would be over. One of his dreams, which he talked about quite frequently, was that all of us would move to Manila and that would be just grand. Unfortunately he died the year before the family did move to Manila. But Ciriaco was with us in spirit and we always remembered him fondly. Dad recalled it was Ciriaco who woke him up when the Japanese patrol was getting closer to the house in Solsona. Did the Japanese know that Father was the commander of the *bolo* men in Solsona? If they did, were they on their way to the house where we resided in Solsona?

When the war was over and many of the evacuees, like us, finally returned to our respective homes, it was time to resume the grind of providing for the family. I found a job, before the high school reopened, as an orderly in a medical dispensary at the United States Air Force base in Gabu, Ilocos Norte. Father found temporary employment at the base also, and was assigned as a foreman with the construction department. The airbase was where some of the Filipino professionals of Ilocos Norte—doctors, lawyers, engineers, teachers, etc.—found work before the economic infrastructure of the country was re-established.

One of the developments in connection with the country's slow return to normalcy was the organization of a private national airline, Far Eastern Airlines Transportation Incorporated (FEATI). It provided a badly needed transportation system between major provinces. Manila served as the hub. Father was appointed Branch Manager of FEATI for the province of Ilocos Norte. That provided employment for a short time with fringe benefits that included free air transportation for immediate members of his family, since there were always empty seats. That is how

I got to visit Basco of Batan Island, in the northernmost province of the Philippines. When a larger airline company, Philippine Air Lines (PAL), was established and took over FEATI, Father decided it was time to resume his college education. He returned to Manila with the whole family, got a civil service assignment with the Bureau of Commerce, and attended Far Eastern University at night. We got an apartment on Lealtad St., in Manila. I remember his coming home late at night; he attended night school after putting in a full day's work. Through that process, he finally earned a Bachelor's degree and, later, a Master's degree in Business Administration. I wish I had told him then how proud I was of him. I hope he knew because, deep in our hearts, we were very proud indeed.

I cannot say much about his singing voice, but his zest for singing more than made up for his voice when he sang love songs with Mother. I listened and remembered the songs, beautiful songs of the 1920s that I still share with my own family in Ann Arbor. Incidentally, these old popular songs have been very much appreciated by the senior citizen residents in two places in Ann Arbor, Hillside Terrace and Lurie Terrace. I play the piano occasionally at both complexes for their evening entertainment.

I can remember the energy with which Father pursued his long productive life. He once visited us in Michigan in the 1960s when he flew from Germany where he had attended a business conference as Assistant Manager of the Philippine Virginia Tobacco Administration. I thought he would be tired from the long trip and would rather spend a restful time with us at the house, and then a leisurely sight-seeing stroll at the campus of the University of Michigan. But mention of the word "golf" seemed to energize him. Without much delay, we were off for a game at the University of Michigan golf course. I trailed behind him as he vigorously pursued his favorite game.

With equal vigor, he pursued his discussion of government policies whenever he had the opportunity. At the table with the family was a favorite forum. We listened respectfully, and that included me, while I was still in high school and in college. Little did he know that while he carried on about how the government should manage its finances, how to deal with dishonest politicians, etc., I was more preoccupied with wondering how to increase my allowance for my next date!

When I was older and more inclined to listen, I recall many times when Dad and I would be discussing issues like foreign trade, government incompetence, corruption, etc., long after the dinner table had been cleared. I was saddened, therefore, when I visited the Philippines to see him just after he had surgery for prostate cancer. He was in his seventies then, and the surgery was not easy on him. He was on his hospital bed at the Philippine General Hospital; he looked tired and was not up to his usual lively and articulate self. Feeble though he was, we exchanged greetings and some small talk. Although I made an effort to banish the thought, I told myself it was probably the last time I would see him alive.

After a few days visit in the Philippines, I returned to Ann Arbor. In about two weeks, I received a short letter from Dad thanking me for my visit and informing me that he was home from the hospital and feeling much better. A month passed, and I received another letter from Dad. This time, it was three pages long in his beautiful penmanship. One page was devoted to the family and to his health, and two pages were devoted to castigating the Philippine government for its incompetence and bungled policies! After reading the long letter, I told my wife, Judy, that I thought Dad was really on his way to a full recovery!

Dad bought my first bicycle, a brand new blue one from the Kairos Bicycle Store on Rizal Street in Laoag, when I was four years old. When it was time to remove the training wheels, he firmly held the back of the seat as he encouraged me to pump on the pedals with my skinny legs so that I could gain speed, maintain equilibrium, and be on my way. "Keep pedaling, son!" I remember his encouragement vividly for it represented how he, a courageous, hard-working and devoted family man, had always wanted his children to be self-reliant and pursue whatever ambitions we had for ourselves.

Dad was born on June 13, 1906. He passed away on March 17, 1998.

Quirico Samonte and Felicidad Segundo's wedding picture. c. 1927.

Lolo Justo Corpuz Samonte carrying the author as a baby, Mother and Father. c. 1929.

Lola Sabina Tumaneng Samonte. c. 1960.

Lola Leoncia
Camacho Segundo.

Lolo Nicolas
Cabanos Segundo.

L to R: Mother, Albino Segundo (*Tio* Bening), Rosalio Segundo (*Tio* Salio), and Desiderio Segundo (*Tio* Deriong).

L to R: *Lola* Leoncia, Esperanza Segundo (Auntie Anching), Miguel Segundo (*Tio* Gli), and *Lola* Tancia (in the back, the younger sister of *Lola* Leoncia).

Auntie Angeles Segundo Weatherhead and Don Weatherhead.

***Tio* Gli and Auntie Alice Dyandante Segundo. c. 1995.**

***Tio* Deriong and Auntie Vicenta Castillo Segundo. c. 1950.**

Auntie Concepcion Mata Segundo and *Tio* Salio at their 60th wedding anniversary celebrated in Las Vegas, Nevada, January 3, 2004.

Auntie Araceli Barba Segundo and *Tio* Bening's wedding picture.

L to R, front and back: Raymundo Versoza (husband of Constancia Samonte, directly behind), Vicente Samonte (husband of Leonor Castro, behind), *Lola* Sabina (*Mama* Ti, behind), Damaso Samonte (husband of Pacita Dancel, behind), Quirico Samonte, Sr. (husband of Felicidad Segundo, behind). c. 1955.

Lolo Nicolas and Lola Leoncia Segundo

Lolo Nicolas Segundo's voice rose in anger as he scolded the hapless client who could not follow the script that *Lolo* was rehearsing in preparation for an interrogation at a court trial. *Lolo* Nicolas was a lawyer, a graduate of the *Escuela de Derecho* in old Manila. He took his profession seriously, and was apparently highly respected not only in our province of Ilocos Norte. He also had clients outside the province including a national business establishment called the *Tabacalera*.

Before I entered grade school, I sometimes sat close by when *Lolo* Nicolas met his clients on the landing at the top of the staircase of the Segundo house. Special clients, like the Spaniards who represented the *Tabacalera*, met in the living room where refreshments were also served. In spite of his anger and impatience with clients who could not follow his directions when he simulated an interrogation in court, he never raised his voice with me. As a matter of fact, we were good friends. I was the first grandchild on both the maternal and paternal sides of my family. Before I entered grade school, and even a short time after, *Lolo* Nicolas and I would, in the afternoon, visit one of his nearby farms. At the end of each school year, it became a ritual for me to show him my report card. He always asked, somewhat jokingly, "Is that the highest in the class?" When he came home from a business trip, he usually brought me a *sarabo* (gift)—be it a toy, a hat or some other item of clothing. In retrospect, I wish I had asked him questions about his parents, his childhood and schooling, how he met *Lola*, and so on. Understandably those questions were not yet a part of my concerns or interests as a small boy.

Based on what I can remember, he enjoyed vegetable gardening, and he also tended to his fruit trees in our yard. These included two mango trees, different varieties of oranges, *chico* (zapote), *atis* (sugar apple), *caimito* (star apple), *pias* (cucumber tree), and four coconut trees. He had close and direct contact with his tenant farmers, especially those who resided on his farm west of Laoag. Sometimes he designed special tools for them. He ventured into some small business enterprises alongside his law practice, and he kept up with current events with his subscription to a Spanish daily, *La Vanguardia*. As a gardener, his main interest was growing vegetables both in the yard of the Segundo house, and at the farms. He encouraged the tenant farmers to plant different crops of vegetables not only for their consumption and marketing, but also for crop rotation, which was good for the soil. But tending to his vegetable garden at home was not always easy. In parts of the yard where land use tended to overlap with *Lola* Leoncia's love for decorative plants, I often overheard scolding coming from the garden when one mistook the other's plants as "weeds" which had been dealt with accordingly. In spite of this "weeding" process, there were obviously enough survivors because *Lolo* Nicolas still had his harvest of *patani* (beans), *paria* (bitter melon), *sili* (pepper), and *carabasa* (squash). *Lola* had her usual blooms of *cadena de amor*, *sampaguita*, *rosal*, yellow bells, poinsettias, *gumamela*, *dama de noche*, and many more.

Lolo Nicolas engaged in a bit of business enterprise as a sideline from his law practice. This included the cultivation of *maguey* plants (used to make rope) by his tenant farmers west of Laoag. I was told there was a large community of workers at the farm with heavy machinery for processing the product. I still saw remnants of huge metal wheels that were mounted on concrete bases a few years later when I visited the farm with *Lolo*. Unfortunately, the market for *maguey* as material for making rope fell when *abaca* fiber turned out to be more durable than *maguey* in salt water. His other project was selling lime which was dug in abundance from one of his farms north of Laoag. There was a demand for it as a mixture for cement, and building contractors bought the lime by the truckloads.

Lolo Nicolas' interest in business dates back to his college days in Manila as a law student. According to *Tio* Salio (Rosalio), *Lolo* Nicolas owned as many as six *calesas* and horses in Manila while he was still a student. These were still used as "taxis" during the the 1890s, the latter part of the Spanish occupation. In this connection, Tio Salio also related a story that *Lolo* Nicolas was at the Luneta to witness the execution of Jose Rizal by the Spanish colonial government. Rizal's execution was the culmination of his conviction for the questionable charge of sedition against the Spanish colonial government. This tragic and cruel event made Rizal a martyr and a hero for the Filipino revolutionary movement against Spain. According to his account, *Lolo* Nicolas was with other students at the execution area, and Rizal looked calm when he arrived. He even greeted the students who came to witness his execution.

Lolo Nicolas' pragmatic and down-to-earth nature, as reflected by his study for a law degree and his business enterprises, was probably too strong to keep him cooped up at the seminary where, at an earlier age, he was once a student. I was told he was a seminarian for a number of years with the intention of becoming a priest. But visiting his girlfriend at night, while still a seminarian, obviously did not fulfill the requirements of monastic discipline. When the school authorities found out about his romantic escapades, he was counseled to explore other vocations. In retrospect, that was just as well or I would not be here to tell about it!

I remember how *Lolo* Nicolas looked whenever he went to the court house, which was only a block away from the Segundo residence. He was always in a white suit, white shirt and black tie, a white straw hat with a stiff brim, and a cane that he carried as part of his outfit. When it got close to the time for him to come home, I would play in the front yard, waiting for him. When I recognized him from a distance, for there were very few men attired like him, I would run out to meet him. He would take my hand and we would walk home together. There was an occasion like this when I thought I saw *Lolo* Nicolas from a distance, properly suited as usual, including the cane. As I got closer to him, I was bewildered for it was not *Lolo*; it was a man who looked very much like my *Lolo* Nicolas! I went back to the house and told my mother I saw someone who looked like *Lolo*. She smiled, but she did not say anything. I learned later that the man I saw that day was *Lolo* Nicolas' son, the result of his clandestine visits to his girlfriend when he was still a student at the seminary. The son became a successful lawyer. It was a strange sight indeed when I saw both of them, sitting across from each other in our living room, discussing some legal matter in a very formal way.

Given his successful legal practice, *Lolo* Nicolas was asked by a number of prominent acquaintances to run for public office, at the provincial level. According to *Tio* Salio, these supporters included Elpidio Quirino, who was then a client of *Lolo* (long before Quirino became President of the Philippines), and Gregorio Aglipay, who was the first Supreme Bishop of the Aglipayan church. Aglipay was also a contemporary of *Lolo* when they were both students at the seminary. After briefly serving as a member of the Provincial Board for Ilocos Norte, *Lolo* apparently found the responsibilities of a public office on the provincial level too time-consuming. He preferred to spend more time with his law practice and business ventures, but he did continue to be in public service on the municipal level. Thus, he allowed his name to be included in the line-up of candidates for councilors for the town of Laoag. More from *Tio* Salio in his letter to me on September 23, 2002:

> Papa was a member of the Laoag Municipal Council for about twenty years without filing his own certificate of candidacy. During those times the party could file on behalf of the candidate, and the party kept doing so. Not surprisingly because many times your *Lolo*, even without campaigning, topped the elections for Laoag councilors.

Lolo Nicolas was ninety-three years old when he passed away on March 17, 1957.

* * *

Dignified and aristocratic in her *terna*, *Lola* Leoncia approached the podium at the stage of the town plaza and delivered an eloquent speech supporting women's suffrage. Although her first language was *Tagalog*, she delivered her speech in flawless *Ilocano*, the dialect in the Ilocos region, and she switched occasionally to Spanish for the benefit of the guests from Manila who were on the stage with her. That was *Lola* Leoncia, the political activist who delivered speeches and debated opponents in public forums, not only in town but throughout the province of Ilocos Norte and whenever she attended national conferences in Manila, sponsored by the Philippine Women's Club. Her political activism included a variety of issues such as taxation and women's rights. She also campaigned for other local, provincial and national candidates for public office. Before the outbreak of World War II she even ran for the office of Vice Mayor of the town of Laoag. She lost that race, but that did not diminish her vigorous and dedicated political participation. It should be noted that she pursued these activities with enthusiasm in the Philippines in the 1930s, before "feminism" gained momentum once again as a popular movement in the United States in the 1960s.

The "Women's Club" was an active organization of middle- and upper-class women of Ilocos Norte, some of whom were the wives of the more prominent men in town. The Segundo House was sometimes a meeting place when *Lola* Leoncia served as a member of its provincial Board of Directors. Thus, the house was occasionally a gathering place of women dressed in their *ternas*. They filled the air with both the fragrance of strong perfume and the smell of sandalwood fans. Sometimes *Lolo* Nicolas would ask me in a whisper, "Is the *cloob* here today?" These were some of the times, including occasions when *Lola* Leoncia assembled her singing friends for their renditions of some arias, that *Lolo* Nicolas and I would sneak out for a trip to the farm. The gathering of the "cloob" or listening to arias was not *Lolo's* thing, especially with the piano placed right next to the wall of his bedroom!

Lola Leoncia had other interests which she pursued with equal vigor. Sometimes the celebration of my birthday in May was a two-day affair, organized by *Lola*. The celebration would start with a day at the farm for a picnic when we would *agborak* at the river. That is, we would harvest fish traps, which consisted of piled-up twigs left for a few months in the shallows of the river before the start of the rainy season. What a delicious picnic that made. There were the usual pork and chicken *adobo*, *igado*, and vegetable *pinakbet* which were prepared at home ahead of time. But the highlight of the picnic was the assortment of freshly caught fish that were grilled; some were simmered as *sinigang*, and others were deliciously spiced *kilawen*. These were prepared right on the river bank. We would be so hungry, especially after swimming and playing games with the bamboo raft, which the men liked to overturn to tease the squealing women. We ate with our hands (*agkammet*) from "plates" fashioned from layers peeled from the stem of a banana plant.

The second day would include a grand luncheon and a dance in the evening with a live orchestra. For all of these events, *Lola* Leoncia was an excellent cook. While two chefs usually came, *Lakay* Chitong and *Lakay* Gorio with their respective assistants, *Lola* Leoncia would cook some of her favorite dishes like *arroz Valenciana*, glazed Chinese ham, fish *ecabeche*, and *leche flan*. She also preserved fruits like *santol*, and these were the occasions when she would serve some of them. Lavish dinners like these were also prepared when special guests were invited from outside the province.

As if being a political activist, excellent cook, and hostess *extraordinaire* were not enough, she was very protective of her family. She cared for those who were sick, and she was a disciplinarian who did not spare the rod! Going to church with her, especially during the Holy Week, one was always rewarded with *gulaman*, a gelatin-like candy served in an eggshell and sold by vendors in front of the church.

While I remember *Lola* Leoncia for her many remarkable skills and achievements, equally memorable was her short temper. One day while *Lola* was tending to her flower garden, a man came to the gate who introduced himself as a cousin of one of the maids. In a somewhat demanding tone, the man informed *Lola* that he wanted to visit his relative. The man made the mistake of adding, perhaps intending to impress or intimidate, that he had just been released from Bilibid Prison. Mention of "Bilibid" would be expected to have an emotional impact comparable to the word "Alcatraz." Bilibid was the national prison in the Philippines for hard-boiled convicts; dealing with a former inmate of Bilibid would normally evoke fear or caution. But not for *Lola* Leoncia. She picked up her leather slipper and slapped the man on the face, saying that "being a former prisoner is nothing to brag about, and I don't like your kind around here. *Fuera*!" The man retreated, dazed and puzzled, I am sure. Later, *Lola's* sons reprimanded her for such an outburst, and reminded her that it was not a very safe thing to do. This temper of *Lola* never spared me, and it was, to some extent, a deterrent to my wayward behavior. But whenever I did receive a paddling from her, it never evoked any bitterness on my part. I knew well enough it was a part of our culture, and I recognized that, in my case, it was always well-deserved. I did play up the howling a bit to exaggerate the pain and suffering, but, sad to say, that did not fool *Lola* Leoncia one bit!

Lola Leoncia passed away when she was ninety years old on November 29, 1979.

* * *

My memories of *Lolo* Nicolas and *Lola* Leoncia would not be complete without remembering my mother's siblings who, in one way or another, influenced me in positive ways and taught me the value of humor. *Lolo* and *Lola* had sixteen children; nine of them survived to adulthood. Starting with the oldest, *Tio* Deriong (Desiderio, Sr.) was never too busy to type my orders for some magic trick gadgets from a company in Detroit, Michigan. Since I was still in the early grades, I relied upon him to identify the item correctly from the catalog, to write the necessary letter, and to go to the post office for a money order even if it was for only twenty-five cents. He addressed the envelope, and determined the right amount of postage. My mother was the second oldest among the nine survivors. *Tio* Bening (Albino), the next born, was definitely the story-teller and the humorist of his family. Gatherings, either with the family or with other guests, were always lively as long as *Tio* Bening was around. *Tio* Salio (Rosalio) was another humorist, but I remember him well because he always asked how I was doing in school and always brought a *sarabo* for me when he came home for vacation from Manila, where he was a law student. He also took me to the movies when I visited Manila during our summer vacations. *Tio* Ating (Nicolas, Jr.) was the body builder who was always flexing his muscles in front of the mirror! I took up body-building myself when I was in college and that was, no doubt, an influence of *Tio* Ating. *Tio* Saring (Nasario) who was fairly independent-minded and not very conventional had the most entertaining stories, that is, once *Lolo* and *Lola* had already left the dinner table. *Tio* Gli (Miguel), about six years older than I, gave me the impression that he had a special way with the ladies. I listened closely when he told stories, just in case there were any helpful hints that might come my way, since I was beginning to become attracted to members of the opposite sex. I thought it probably helped, too, that he had a powerful and well modulated singing voice. He sometimes sang "Ave Maria" in church. Auntie Anching (Esperanza) and Auntie Angeles were closer to my age. They sometimes included me in their playhouse activities when I was of preschool age until, one day, in an act of revenge, I "massacred" their dolls while they were in school. I cut off the dolls' heads with Mother's sewing scissors. I guess they eventually forgave me for that. When Auntie Anching started teaching in the public schools, and Auntie Angeles was a nurse at the University of Santo Tomas Hospital, I would visit them once in a while for a little "pocket money" when I was still in college. I also remember Auntie Angeles for other reasons; we were very much alike in some ways. She had made her share of mischief, including the time she almost drowned at the Laoag River when she was still in grade school. This happened, she recalled, when she and her friends decided to go "wading" in the river one weekend. She also told me about being reprimanded by the nuns at the University of Santo Tomas for hiding under her bed with another classmate in order to avoid the dormitory residents' daily recitation of the rosary. In spite of these infractions, she was an honor student when she finished elementary school, and graduated *Cum Laude* when she received her nursing degree at the University of Santo Tomas. Only three of the siblings survive today: *Tio* Salio, *Tio* Gli, and Auntie Angeles.

Looking back over the years, we have been a closely-knit extended family that, indeed, up to this day, still enjoys recalling happy and treasured memories during those rare occasions when the surviving members get together. The sad memories are locked in our hearts as part of the burden we share in our journey through life.

Going to the farm with Lolo Nicolas

Lolo Justo and Lola Sabina Samonte

Under the shade of the huge tamarind tree or beneath the trellis of the grapevine, the turkeys would sometimes crowd around me and *Lolo* Justo Samonte, my paternal grandfather, when we fed them with left-over rice and old bread. They were so tame, and the toms would show off with a display of their tail feathers. As a three-year-old, I thought the turkeys were fun to feed, not like the geese that would stretch out their long necks towards me like a snake! *Lolo* Justo was already in his eighties when he spent time with me in his garden, which was like a zoo!

There were Guinea fowl in an enclosed screened structure in one corner of the yard, and at least half a dozen geese in another fenced off section. The ducks, chickens and turkeys had the run of the rest of the garden. I think part of the wing feathers of the geese and ducks were trimmed periodically to keep them from flying away! We also had pigeons, and they flew in and out of their house, which looked like a mini apartment complex with a lot of little doors. We made sure there was always food and water for them so they would come back. They sometimes brought back some of their friends with them!

A herd of sheep were in another part of the yard, which had a roofed structure that provided shade from the sun and protection from the rain. They were let out every day to forage elsewhere. Along with the pigs, dogs and cats, this was our private zoo. This was my play area as the first grandchild, a place that *Lolo* Justo and I shared when we fed the turkeys. What an enchanting place it was; I cannot overemphasize the pleasures it provided me. It was also a setting where I got to know more about my paternal grandfather as a caring and gentle man, and his kindness to the "creatures of God," as he called them. He made sure everyone in the flock got its share of the food.

I was seven years old when *Lolo* Justo passed away on October 8, 1935. He was eighty-eight years old. Because of the relatively short time I had known him while I was just a small boy, I have supplemented my recollections with an unpublished manuscript by Uncle Damaso, an older brother of my father, which includes some of his observations about *Lolo*. According to Uncle Damaso, *Lolo* was one of eight children. Their father was Juan Samonte, and their mother was Perfecta Corpuz. Great-grandfather Juan was a Spanish *mestizo*, who served as an officer in the Spanish Army. He was designated as a *Caballero* after his service with the military.

> Our father, Justo Samonte (my *Lolo* Justo), was the fifth of eight children, namely, Pio, Gregorio, Francisco, Marcelo, Justo, Ildefonsa, Tito and Irineo. He was about five feet eight inches, much taller than the average man of his time. He was the quiet type, never given to too much talking. He was temperate in his habits and very religious. He never failed to go to church on Sunday. He belonged to a group of elderly citizens that supported the *Aglipayan* Church, otherwise known as the Philippine Independent Church. He never failed to pray upon the ringing of the vesper bell, and always had a prayer of thanks in Spanish after supper.

* * *

Grandmother Sabina Tumaneng (*Lola* Sabina), according to uncle Damaso,

> ...was the eldest of ten children, namely, Sabina, Susana, Fructosa, Barbara, Mamerta, Victoria, Agripina, Hilarion, Benito, and Servillano... Mother was a vigorous hardworking woman. She had good health for practically the entire stretch of her long life, save the time she manifested incipient signs of tuberculosis that miraculously healed and never showed any signs of recurrence. She came from a family that was devotedly Roman Catholic; but she was not religious, if we go by the regularity or rather rarity of her going to church. She was not a Sunday itinerant for spiritual salvation. The only time I noticed mother feeling some compulsion to put on her Sunday clothes was during church holidays, particularly during Holy Week. But unlike most people, she never essayed a full week observance. One day of penance, perhaps, was enough to replenish her spiritual store for the rest of the year.

My recollections of *Lola* Sabina are equally personal, but from the perspectives of an adoring grandson. I remember her long gray hair, shiny with a touch of coconut oil, combed neatly towards the back of her head and knotted into a bun. She was not given to casual or idle chatter. She spoke sparingly but with thought and her friends listened with respect.

But to her many grandchildren who knew her as *Lola* Sabina, she was loving and playful. We looked forward to visiting her almost everyday. She was always there for us, ready with her stories, and the evening would come alive with enchanted gardens and haunted mountains. We would huddle close to her on the bamboo floor of her *nipa* hut, and we would be entertained by the magic of *Lola* Sabina's stories.

Story-telling by Lola Sabina

Our young imaginations provided color, sound and panoramic vistas that unfolded in our mind's eye. With cousins Erning, Romeo, Sigrid, Ruth, Evelyn, and Josephine, we listened to *Lola* Sabina's version of *Juan Sadot*, that proverbial lazy boy whose adventures were so popular they were also narrated in different dialects to children in various regions of the Philippines. In Juan Sadot, the ending was usually a lesson on the negative consequences of being lazy.

Her stories about Diego Silang (1730–1763) were about the heroism of an Ilocano from La Union who incited a rebellion against the Spaniards to protest high taxes and involuntary labor. Diego Silang was later assassinated. His wife, Gabriela Silang, took over the localized rebellion by leading her late husband's forces to battle. She was eventually captured and hanged by the Spaniards in 1763. Diego Silang is considered "the precursor of the reformist and nationalist movements which were to sweep the country (Philippines) more than a century after his death." (*Filipino Heritage*, 1978, pp. 1322–1327)

In the realm of fantasy, *Biag ni Lam-Ang* (Life of Lam-Ang) was one of our favorites. "The Ilokano epic *Biag ni Lam-Ang* is believed to be among the oldest Filipino poems in existence. Some scholars, like H. Otley Beyer and Renwald Brandstetter, assign it a pre-Hispanic date." (*Filipino Heritage*, p. 1506) It deals with the birth of *Lam-Ang* after his father was taken captive by an enemy tribe, the child's gift of speech, apparent even at birth, how he fought adversaries with the use of amulets and magic in his search for his father, and how *Lam-Ang* was resurrected after he died in battle.

Regarding *Lola* Sabina's cooking, I was fond of *sinuman*, a gelatinous rice dish which was steamed and simmered with freshly squeezed coconut milk and molasses. When she prepared *sinuman*, she was assisted by one of her helpers *Baket* Sabel or *Baket* Matti. When all the chores were done for the day, they would get the ingredients ready. Meanwhile Erning, Romeo and I would be getting ready to settle down for the night in *Lola* Sabina's hut. I would hear the grating of the coconut from the *igad*, a round serrated blade mounted on wood fashioned from a tree branch that was shaped like a tripod. While the coconut was grated, the gelatinous rice was steamed. I could tell how the *sinuman* was progressing because when the coconut milk started to reduce there was that unmistakable smell of *ladek*, the browned residue from the coconut milk. The residue was just two or three tablespoons full, but I thought nothing could match its aroma and flavor, especially when sprinkled with sugar. As I began to fall asleep, I would fade away with the thought that I would have *ladek* and *sinuman* when I got up for breakfast.

Lola Sabina always made enough for all members of the extended family. A plate of *sinuman* would be brought by the houseboy to my mother and father's home, and there were deliveries to Uncle Damaso's,

Uncle Vicente's, and Auntie Tansing's family. We would have *sinuman* when mangoes were in season; we usually ate the two together for *merienda*. Sometimes we had *sinuman* with Auntie Cristina's home-made chocolate, which was served in little cups.

Although my evenings with *Lola* Sabina were over seventy years ago, I can still visualize an oasis of tranquility, and a reminder that wholesome pleasures can come from simple things. I remember *Lola* Sabina's dignity, how it radiated from her, and her ready smile for the grandchildren.

Lola Sabina passed away on June 23, 1967. She was ninety-nine years old and six months.

Mama Ti

One clear night in Laoag just after sunset, *Mama* Ti (Auntie Cristina) called cousins Erning, Romeo, and me to look out of the living room window. Pointing to the sky close to the horizon, she said, "That is the Southern Cross." Unable to recognize it right away amidst other points of reflected light, she narrowed our search to four bright stars which, sure enough, were shaped like a cross! Another night just after dinner, she assembled us on the *asotea* (open patio) to look almost straight up to see *Cassiopeia, Orion* and the Little Dipper. At grade school age, it was fascinating indeed to know that there were such formations in the sky and that they seemed to maintain their position in relation to one another every night! I was less keen, however, when she asked us if we could wake up at five o'clock in the morning so that we could see the Big Dipper and the North Star! But that was *Mama* Ti, the dedicated professional educator, or

Astronomy lessons by Mama Ti on the *asotea (bansag)*

Maestra, as she was always addressed respectfully by the people in town and by our tenant farmers.

Mama Ti, the oldest sister of eight children in my father's family, was no ordinary educator. As early as the 1930s, for example, she was a supervisor of the public schools, a position traditionally held by men. She was assigned at one time as school supervisor in the town of Bangui, in the northern part of Ilocos Norte along the

China Sea. While on that assignment, I was told that she rode on horseback when she visited less accessible schools under her jurisdiction.

Every summer, my family would take the bus and stay with *Mama* Ti for vacation. She rented a spacious one-story house with a large balcony overlooking the town plaza. In the yard there was an assortment of citrus trees. The town of Bangui and its vicinity were known for their orange groves, and oranges from that region were sold throughout the province. Even more exciting for me, a pre-schooler at that time, was that we were only about a ten-minute walk from the China Sea. I could hear the roaring waves day and night, and we walked to the beach to bathe every morning. There was a clear and shallow fresh-water stream that flowed into the sea where the children played and bathed. The adults braved the pounding waves. After our morning bath and play by the sea, *Mama* Ti would have a huge bowl of peeled oranges and bananas mixed with evaporated milk and sugar waiting for us! There was always the dependable *pandesal*, a crusty breakfast roll, and sometimes *ensemada*, a buttery twist sprinkled with sugar from the local bakery. This was accompanied by *Mama* Ti's famous hot chocolate which she made herself from fresh cacao beans.

Although *Mama* Ti was a pioneer, having served as a public school supervisor in the 1930s, she later requested to be reassigned to Laoag at the lower rank of principal. This meant no more horseback riding but, more importantly, it meant she would be closer to her family. As the oldest among *Lolo* Justo and *Lola* Sabina's eight children and being single, perhaps she always had that sense of responsibility to her extended family. This probably explains her affectionate name of "*Mama* Ti" to her many nieces and nephews.

After her re-assignment to our hometown, Laoag, *Mama* Ti served as principal for Shamrock Elementary School, then later for Central Elementary School, and finally for Gabaldon Elementary School. I was enrolled at Central from grade one through five while *Mama* Ti was the school principal. I transferred to Gabaldon for my sixth grade when *Mama* Ti was assigned to that school. The idea was to insure that I would be under the watchful eye of *Mama* Ti; she had the reputation of being a strong leader as well as a disciplinarian. I think this was particularly reassuring to Mom and Dad since they thought I did not do too well in kindergarten and I was developing a reputation for getting other kids into all kinds of mischief. Thus, *Mama* Ti would provide, they hoped, that strong "guiding hand" that they felt I needed.

She gave me guidance all right, in the form of a foot-long wooden ruler that she applied expertly on the palm of my hands whenever she thought such punishment was warranted. She did not "spare the rod" and there was no debate about whether it hurt my "self-esteem," psyche or whatever educational psychologists might be concerned with nowadays. Fully aware that I had disregarded some rules that everybody else was expected to follow, I accepted my punishment without complaining. It was, in effect, a clear enough differentiation between right and wrong, as viewed by my teachers and elders, and that was good enough for me. Simplistic perhaps, but it provided consistency, integrity and direction during my childhood. There was time enough in later years for me to interact more critically and constructively within my social environment so that I could still shape my own individual values.

One of the projects *Mama* Ti undertook as school administrator was her periodic confiscation of slingshots from the school boys. As an *aficionado* of slingshots, I was also subject to the surprise "sweeps" that were conducted by the teachers. Long before the publication of *Silent Spring* by Rachel Carson in 1962, *Mama* Ti was a strong advocate of protection and kindness to animals with emphasis on birds as "the friends of man." Hence, her regular campaign against slingshots!

Frequent trips with *Mama* Ti to the Samonte farm in the village of Capacacan, in the town of Banna, was a treat for her nieces and nephews. On the way to the village, *Mama* Ti always stopped at the bakery to buy a large bag of *pandesal*, *pandesito*, and *biscotso* for the children of the tenant farmers. If any of the tenant farmers needed some medicine from town, she made sure she had that, too.

At the farm, *Mama* Ti encouraged the tenants to develop their own rules of conduct for dealing with infractions, such as stray animals that got into someone else's garden. She also helped them develop rules for the election of leaders by the tenant farmers. *Mama* Ti brought improvements to the farm to help deal with sanitation—she showed tenants how to build properly covered latrines and how to dispose of garbage by burning it or covering it with earth to minimize breeding places for flies. To increase productivity, she discussed with the tenant farmers seed selection, crop rotation, and the recycling of plant cuttings to use as fertilizer. She also invited a relative who was a horticulturist to demonstrate techniques of grafting and budding fruit trees to combine two or more varieties or to hasten fruit bearing time. To me, *Mama* Ti's approach to running the farm was more persuasive than mandatory, more democratic and less authoritarian than the practices of other landowners in the province. To the tenant farmers, she indeed lived up to her title as *Maestra*.

For our family, *Mama* Ti is also fondly remembered for her chocolate, *polboron*, and *tupig*. Making the chocolate was a real production that started with the purchase of the cacao beans from the local Chinese store, and culminated with hot chocolate that was served in small cups during *merienda* (mid-afternoon refreshment). Once the beans were brought home from the store, *Mama* Ti and *Nana* Aning, the woman who always came to help make chocolate, went to work. They sunned the cacao beans to dry thoroughly, removed the shells, roasted the beans in a clay pot with constant stirring, and then ground the cacao several times until it turned into a thick oily paste. At this point the strong smell of chocolate filled the house. By coincidence, that was also the time when the little nieces and nephews would begin to congregate in the kitchen. Coincidence, or was it like humming birds that show up when the flowers are in bloom? At any rate, at this stage, there was no tasting allowed for the chocolate was still bitter. Sugar was carefully measured and mixed into the chocolate paste. The mixture was then shaped into little round molds and dried on banana leaves. When fully dried, these molds were stored and used as needed. That was *Mama* Ti's famous chocolate, worthy, I am sure, of Jose Rizal's *chocolate eh!*

Her retirement from the public schools did not consign *Mama* Ti to the rocking chair. She continued to assist several nephews and nieces who needed help, whether it was counseling or a little financial help, and she still found time to be active in the Girl Scouts organization of Ilocos Norte.

During one of my later trips to the Philippines, *Mama* Ti turned 101 years old. She was still mentally alert, got around the house unaided and even attended the parties held at her place. I had a chance to chat with her. "I am glad you became a teacher because it is a noble profession," she told me. After a long thoughtful pause, she continued, "But I never thought you would become one." I asked her why. With a twinkle in her eyes, she looked at me and said, "Because you were so naughty!" She had not forgotten! And I will never forget my remarkable *Mama* Ti: her professionalism, her pioneering spirit, her kindness, her commitment to a more democratic way of relating to our tenant farmers, and her tireless effort to improve the tenant farmers' lives. She did all that while still loving and caring for her many nieces and nephews, who depended upon her as an exceptional role model.

Mama Ti passed away in December, 1998, at the age of 103.

Tio Papa

With conviction and eloquence, Uncle Damaso (*Tio Papa* to his nephews and nieces) made use of his "privilege hour" in the Philippine Congress to challenge the wisdom of granting general amnesty to guerrilla members who were accused of crimes against humanity committed during World War II. As a member of the first postwar Congress, Uncle Damaso had the opportunity and platform to condemn what many Ilocanos regard as a shameful chapter in our history, when self-styled guerrillas took advantage of war conditions to loot, rape and murder their own countrymen. It was no surprise, therefore, that there were sometimes armed conflicts between those guerrilla units that were endorsed by the exiled provincial government and those who later came from outside Ilocos Norte during the war and organized themselves as guerrillas. It was some members of the latter group that were accused of atrocities.

For the first group of guerrillas, Uncle Damaso attended to their wounded whenever he could. On one of these occasions, I remember late one night, we heard knocking at the door. It was a "runner," as messengers of the guerrillas were then called. He asked if Uncle Damaso could come with him, for there were wounded *guerrilleros* just outside the Japanese-occupied and barricaded town of Laoag. I carried Uncle Damaso's bag and accompanied him as we slipped away from the town under cover of darkness. When we reached the house where the wounded were assembled, it was a gruesome sight indeed. Some of the *guerrilleros* were already dead with multiple cuts on their faces and limbs. *Tio Papa* was not unmindful of the risk he was taking in attending to the wounded *guerrilleros*. Did the Japanese know or suspect anything? The Japanese Military Police did imprison Uncle Damaso for a few days for interrogation, but that was long before that night we went out to help the *guerrilleros*.

Regarding his imprisonment, Uncle Damaso speculated that the following happened. The Japanese Military Police arrested a friend who was in contact with a guerrilla unit west of Laoag. The Japanese could have extracted information from this friend, information about other people in town who may have had knowledge about the resistance movement. There were others arrested after that, including two of my maternal uncles, Desiderio Segundo and Miguel Segundo. They happened to be the brothers-in-law of a guerrilla commander, Feliciano Madamba, who was married to Auntie Anching, my mother's younger sister.

The suspected informant was later executed by the Japanese, but Uncle Damaso's, Desiderio's and Miguel's lives were spared. Madamba was later captured by the Japanese and probably executed since we never saw him again.

Tio Papa related a story after he was released from prison. He recalled that when the Japanese took him to a darkened cell, he thought he was alone. As his eyes adjusted to the dark, he noticed what he thought was a crumpled pile in one corner. Upon investigation, it turned out to be a badly bruised man. After checking that the man was still alive, he was taken aback to discover it was Mariano Marcos, the father of Ferdinand Marcos who would later become President of the Philippines. *Tio Papa* recalled that in the last conversation he had with Mariano Marcos in that prison cell, he requested Uncle Damaso to please check the swelling on the leg of one of Marcos' horses. In this connection, I should add that during the war I had accompanied *Tio Papa* horseback riding. Sometimes it was just the two of us. Other times we rode with Mariano Marcos, who used to keep four beautiful horses at his stable in Laoag. After *Tio Papa* saw him at the Military Police prison, what happened to Mariano Marcos? Regalado Trota Jose notes in *A Chronology of Ilocos Norte History* that "Mariano Marcos is believed to have perished in the hands of renegade guerrillas." (p. 22) It was rumored also that some of the top Filipino officials who were associated with the Japanese-sponsored provincial government in Ilocos Norte fled with the Japanese, and that, for one reason or another, they were never heard from again. Whether this was what really happened, the rumor did provide some closure to a dark chapter in our history.

Given the atrocities to which the people were subjected by some self-styled guerrillas, as experienced in the Ilocos region of Luzon, *Tio Papa* saw that the passage of the bill for General Amnesty for guerrillas would be a gross miscarriage of justice. In opposing the bill, it should be noted that he took a stand against the position of his own political party, the Liberal Party, and against Manuel Roxas, who was then the first President of the Republic of the Philippines. For a freshman congressman, taking a stand against his political party and the President was probably not a recipe for political longevity. But this particular episode epitomized *Tio Papa's* idea of public service and his belief in standing up for what he considered honorable. This philosophy guided his actions when he was elected as governor and congressman of Ilocos Norte and later, when he was appointed Under-Secretary of Health under President Garcia. The 14th Annual Asssembly of the World Health Organization also elected him as one of its three Vice Presidents.

I remember my experience when I needed to extend my visa and those of other members of my family by one day when we visited the Philippines in 1966. The clerk wanted me to pay him extra money before he would do the paper work. Not wanting to be a party to government corruption, I raised my voice and told the clerk to "Go to hell," loud enough for other clerks in his office to hear. They looked over in my direction. The wrong date on our visa was an error made by the immigration official who had stamped our passports when we arrived in the Philippines for our visit. The date stamped was one day before of the arrival of the SS President Wilson, on which we had a round trip booking to return to the United States. When I called the immigration official's attention to the wrong date, he acknowledged the error. Instead of correcting it then, he told me there would be no problem adjusting it when it was time for us to leave. Given the excitement of our visit to the Philippines (my wife and children were meeting my family for the first time), it was easy to forego the immediate resolution of what I thought was a minor clerical error. But was it intentional? When I mentioned the incident at the government office to Uncle Damaso, he was very angry, as I expected. "Don't give a single cent to those s.o.b.s," he thundered! Thus, my first visit to the Philippines after an absence of twelve years ended on a rather sordid note with a demand for a bribe by a government clerk! Instead of giving in to petty corruption, my parents helped us by providing the extra fare for plane tickets to Hong Kong so we could board the SS President Wilson in Hong Kong for the return trip to the United States. The extra fare to Hong Kong was, of course, much more than what the clerk expected from us, which was probably just a few pesos for lunch or cigarettes.

Aside from his public life, his many nephews and nieces referred to Uncle Damaso affectionately as *Tio Papa*, and for good reason. I remember him showing us how to make

French toast and pancakes, how to observe gun safety when he took us hunting, and how to bait the hook when we went fishing.

Best of all for me was when he let me care for and ride "Snowball," a handsome yearling colt. I was fourteen years old when I met "Snowball," the son of "Mama Ines," the mare that Uncle Damaso pastured in *Barrio* Cataban for breeding. He was taller than the native horses because "Mama Ines" was bred with the stallion that the government kept at the breeding station in Biding, Dingras. "Snowball" held his head high, and he was tame and friendly. I rode him in the afternoons toward the countryside, sometimes with uncle Damaso, and sometimes by myself.

With all the good times I had while riding "Snowball," Uncle Damaso told me the horse would probably bond with me more if I helped take care of him. I think it was his way of telling me that with pleasure comes work and responsibility. Those responsibilities included walking the horse after a ride, brushing his coat and mane, cutting the grass for his feed, mixing the rice bran with water and a little bit of molasses, and cleaning the stable! I made sure that the saddles and bits were kept clean and shiny. I also helped hold "Snowball" when they changed his shoes. The reward for all this work was riding "Snowball" early in the morning when I would take him to the river for his bath and, after our swim, ride him bareback, racing the wind along the river bank.

One afternoon, Uncle Damaso was mending his old shirt while Erning and I were playing chess nearby. He commented there was something noble about mending an old article of clothing, done well to show skill and respect for the material, and later worn with pride. Over the years I have also taken pride in wearing some of my clothes from the years when I was still in college, provided they still fit! However, a few trips to my friend Bruno, the tailor, did not always do the trick. Bruno jokingly said he did not think it was a good idea for him to keep letting out my trousers. "You must diet and exercise." Bruno reprimanded. So much for being noble and building character, I thought I had better listen to Bruno.

Uncle Damaso was a reader. He read regularly before he took his siesta in the afternoon, and again late at night before going to sleep. I sometimes browsed through his bookshelves when I was in high school. As a medical doctor, he had the usual medical textbooks. But there were other selections that I can remember including Marx and Engel's *Communist Manifesto*, Gibran's *The Prophet*, Boccaccio's *Decameron*, a law book by Justice Cardozo, Darwin's *The Origin of Species* and some books by Joseph Conrad. I do not recall the other selections, but the titles I do remember indicate, I think, a person with a wide range of interests beyond his medical profession.

As I look back at the life of a man who tried to contribute his share to establish the "good society," I sometimes wonder what his private thoughts were about the conflicts he encountered between his ideals and the limitations of a traditional agricultural society that was dominated by elite wealthy landowners. For someone who sacrificed his time and personal resources to serve his country in so many capacities, it must have been sickening to him to read about the assassinations of promising political leaders, some of whom he knew personally. I remember how angry he would become to read about corrupt public officials who took advantage of their positions to plunder the public treasury and get away with it. How disappointing it must have been for him when he legally fought election frauds in Ilocos Norte, and the fight he mounted to challenge voting irregularities was not going anywhere.

His personal experience with public service was no doubt a very frustrating challenge that paralleled the task of the Philippines, a country struggling to fulfill its commitment to a truly representative form of government, relatively free from the bias of vested interests, especially those of the landlords and of the Roman Catholic Church. I hope he rationalized that his struggle was a necessary component of a painful beginning. I also like to believe that the ideals of leaders like Uncle Damaso can be re-ignited to provide light and guidance to what appears to be a dark and challenging future for the Philippines. His belief in the rule of law, his faith in the sanctity of the ballot and his uncompromising stand against corruption are worth striving for if the country is to survive with dignity, regain the faith of its people and the respect of the world community.

Tio Salio

It must be an awkward moment for the traveler who has just arrived home and, as he unpacks, is surrounded by eager relatives expecting a *sarabo*. A Filipino tradition of long standing, the *sarabo* is a gift that is expected from a relative who has come home from a long journey. It probably started as a way of reinforcing the extended family network, but it can be an expensive practice that has actually discouraged a few Filipino-Americans from visiting the Philippines as frequently as they would like because of the additional expense of that expected *sarabo*. I wonder if *Tio* Salio ever felt uncomfortable when we crowded into his bedroom as he opened his *maleta* (suitcase) after arriving in Laoag for the summer or Christmas vacation from Manila where he was a law student. While my wide-eyed attention was focused on his *maleta* as he peeled out one item of clothing after another, he talked about the crowded train ride and the transfer to the

"Norlutran" bus (Northern Luzon Transportation) at the province of La Union. This was an interesting enough topic for me but was overshadowed by my anxiety wondering what pleasant surprise he might have had in his suitcase for me, a young kid still in early elementary school.

Looking back, I should not have worried too much. He always had something for me, even if some of the other relatives did not always get a *sarabo*. My favorite *sarabo* was a cap gun, a prized item for a boy my age who was familiar with cowboy stars like Tom Tyler, Buck Jones, Johnny Mack Brown, Gene Autry and Bob Steele. I mention this for it was very much like *Tio* Salio to be considerate, full of good humor, and always encouraging me to do well in school.

Another interesting time at the dinner table was when *Tio* Salio was newly arrived from that far away and exciting city of Manila. His stories held everyone's attention. He talked about the excitement of student activism at the Luneta, where the students would gather in the thousands. He recounted the tense rivalries between universities, the glamorous student leaders like Carmen Planas, and some of the debates at the university. Can you imagine how all these stories fired my imagination, thinking about how great it would be to be a university student in Manila? Fortunately I did not have to wait too long to go to the big city.

A couple of times when I was still in elementary school, my mother would entrust me to her cousin Terio, a bus driver for the Maria de Leon bus company of Laoag, when I would make that trip to Manila for the long summer vacation. About ten pesos were securely sewed by Mother into my pocket, money to spend for the duration of the summer with my *Lola Ubing* (Young Grandmother), the younger sister of *Lola* Leoncia. *Lola Ubing* or *Lola* Tancia, her real name, lived with her brother, *Lolo* Colas (same first name as my *Lolo* Nicolas Segundo). *Lolo* Colas was a *makinista*, a projectionist, at the Avenue Theatre, one of the big, air-conditioned movie houses in Manila. It was exciting to go with *Lolo* Colas to that tall building, the Avenue Theatre, which was located on the busy *Avenida* Rizal. What was memorable about accompanying *Lolo* Colas was going up the elevator in what must have been, to the eyes of a young *probinciano* like me, at least a ten-story building, looking at those huge machines in the projection room, and being introduced to the ticket seller and ushers who were all, I thought, beautiful *mestizas*. They were so good-looking I even entertained the thought that I would not mind being married to anyone of them right then and there, even if I was only ten years old. Anyway, my infatuation with the ticket seller and ushers soon faded away when the main feature started. It was the premier showing of *Pinocchio* in Technicolor!

While I was in Manila for the summer, *Tio* Salio was never too busy to visit on weekends to take me out (we would include Auntie Angeles if she was also in Manila for vacation). I would make my selection to see one of those "whole serials." That was when the movie houses would show several weekly episodes all at one time. The shows that I could choose to see included "The Lone Ranger," "Undersea Kingdom," "The Shadow," and "Flash Gordon."

Before returning to *Lola* Ubing's apartment, *Tio* Salio and I usually ended up at a *halo halo* (fresh and candied fruit with milk and crushed ice) stand or at a Magnolia Dairy shop where we would have a glass of chocolate milk or any of the different flavors of ice cream, like *macapuno, ube, mango, ananka*, vanilla or chocolate.

Summer trips to Manila for me ended with the outbreak of World War II. The Segundos, including Mother and my sisters, evacuated to the Segundo farm in Surate, Dingras. Each family was assigned a *nipa* hut. *Tio* Salio stayed with Mother and Father, and he continued to live with us even after we moved to *Barrio* Katebbegan at the farm of Emilio and Trinidad Mata and, later, when we moved to the town of Solsona. I think staying with us was more relaxing for *Tio* Salio, and he enjoyed discussions with Dad about current events. He also sometimes accompanied the *guerrilleros* when they went out on horseback to patrol the surrounding areas. It was a safe enough venture, I suppose, and helpful for *Tio* Salio who, I am sure, found the war years burdensome and monotonous.

My family stayed in Solsona during the war for about three years. It was also during that time that love bloomed between *Tio* Salio and Concepcion Mata, later to become my Auntie Conching. She was one of three lovely daughters of Emilio and Trinidad Mata of Solsona. Earlier, it was through the kindness and generosity of the Mata family that we stayed at their family farm in *Barrio* Katebbegan when Father and Mother decided to move away from the guerrilla headquarters in the Segundo farm in Surate, Dingras.

The end of the war opened up a fresh start for everybody. It was back to school for me, work and studies for Dad, politics for Uncle Damaso, and law practice plus politics for *Tio* Salio, who eventually pursued a distinguished career in the judicial branch of the newly independent Republic of the Philippines. Included among the different positions he held were: Justice of the Peace for Solsona, 1946–1954; Second Assistant Provincial Fiscal of Ilocos Norte, 1954–1962; First Assistant Provincial Fiscal of Ilocos Norte, 1962–1971; Acting Provincial Fiscal of Ilocos Norte, 1964–1965; Judge of the Court of First Instance of Pangasinan, for a number of years from 1971; and Regional Trial Court Judge of the Manila Branch, from 1983 up to his retirement in 1985. He also served as a faculty member of the College of Law of the Divine Word College of Ilocos Norte for seven years. After retirement from his judicial duties, he continued to practice law until 2002.

A visit to Solsona in 1966 with Judy and my two daughters, Cristina and Cynthia, revived pleasant memories of generous and kind friends in an idyllic setting. *Tio* Salio, Auntie Conching and the Mata family prepared a memorable trip for us to their Katebbegan farm and a picnic to the beautiful Karinkin River. At the farm, they thoughtfully arranged a number of fun activities for the children like the harvest of sugar cane, extraction of juice through a primitive press powered by a *carabao*, and a ride for the children on the *ulnas*, a small wooden sled pulled by a *carabao*. Judy even dared to ride bareback on a *carabao*!

The following day, a picnic was arranged at Karinkin River. It is situated east of Solsona in a ruggedly beautiful setting. The scenery was dominated by a clear, cool spring-fed river. Framed by luxuriant vegetation, it was free from any traces of urban development, noise or pollution. What could be a better place to enjoy the fellowship and hospitality of good friends, and the unmatched flavors of *tinono nga paltat* (grilled cat fish), *tinenneb nga dalag* (grilled mudfish with vinegar, pepper and ginger sauce), *pinakbet* (mixed vegetable stew made as good as only the Ilocanos can make it), and *lechon* (whole pig roasted on a spit, usually rotated by a couple of volunteers who are fortified by a bottle of *basi*, sugar cane wine). As if the visit to Katebbegan and the picnic at Karinkin were not enough, *Tio* Salio and Auntie Conching arranged an evening dance on their patio. Music was provided by none other than Cosme. Remember, he was the blind violinist who, with his music, gave so much beauty and comfort to the people in Solsona during the war. I cannot say enough about the pleasures that our friends in Solsona have unselfishly shared with us all these years, and I cannot thank them enough. Their love and kindness shall forever remain in my thoughts.

As I reminisce about times past, I can feel with *Tio* Salio what he expressed in his recent letter to me:

> The pieces you wrote took me back to memory lane to those good old days when we were still young, living in complete abandon, not minding what will happen next. To me, who is now in the twilight of my life, reading things like these make me feel young again and feel happy recalling those people who were close to us who have now left this world.

Tio Gli

Tio Gli pedaled furiously on the bicycle as I hung on to him while I sat in the back, balanced precariously. It was just after dinner in the evening and we were on our way to Sarrat, about five miles away on a rough gravel road. It was hard going for *Tio* Gli, I am sure, but since we were on our way to visit his girl friend in Sarrat, I am positive the incentive was worth all the effort for him. As for me, I was not sure why I went along for the ride, and the question gained more significance to me as I felt, ever more keenly, the bumps on the road. I was about twelve then, and I must have tagged along as an apprentice.

You might be wondering how much parental supervision young Filipino boys had, being out on the road to another town at that time of the night. *Tio* Gli took care of that! Since *Lola* Leonica was then a candidate for public office, I remember *Tio* Gli volunteered to go around the town of Laoag after dinner to distribute some of *Lola's*

To Sarrat with *Tio* Gli

campaign posters. I am sure what appeared as thoughtfulness on our part was probably also regarded by our elders as an early and promising interest in the political process. He was given permission, and I was even allowed to go along with him! Unfortunately for them, the elders did not know we were on our way to Sarrat, which was outside the jurisdiction for *Lola's* candidacy. In retrospect, if the other political supporters of *Lola* were like *Tio* Gli and me, I hope that was not the reason *Lola* lost that election!

We finally got there. Tired and dusty as I was, I readily complied when *Tio* Gli and his girl friend suggested that I could go to sleep, if I wanted to. I thought they were so considerate and kind! So much for being an apprentice, for I promptly fell asleep, and was awakened when it was time to go back to Laoag a few hours later!

Since I was the first born grandchild in the Segundo as well as in the Samonte family, *Tio* Gli was the closest I had to an older brother since he was only a few years older than I. Thus, I learned a lot from him during our younger years, such as how to make a top from hard wood, like *narra* or *palogapig*, how to select the right kind of wood for sling shots, how to spin the yo-yo, how to throw the *lipay*, and how to make a canon out of a bamboo tube for New Year's fireworks. I look back at those years when we entertained ourselves with simple and home-made toys. I am convinced making our own toys made us more creative, appreciative of simple things, and more inclined to look after our toys with care. From this perspective I tend to subscribe to the view that more is not necessarily better. When I witness some of the affluent kids in the United States who are inundated with toys during Christmas, I have wondered if they are any happier than we were with toys which we made ourselves. I am sure I share those memories with *Tio* Gli, who sometimes included me when he played with the other boys his age in the neighborhood.

Tio Gli had a desk that had a top that was hinged and could open up. When he opened it I was always fascinated to look at his assorted collections of knickknacks: an old knife, a yo-yo, a wooden ruler, rubber bands, a slingshot, colorful bottle caps, marbles, pictures of movie stars, little scraps of leather for slingshots, etc. It was like a treasure chest to me, and I suspect it was also like that to *Tio* Gli when he was still in elementary school. He occasionally took his treasures out, probably like Silas Marner, a fictional character I remember from our high school literature class, who liked to count his money once in a while.

Hanging on the wall in *Tio* Gli's closet was his pair of roller skates. These really intrigued me, and I must admit I could not refrain from trying them out on the *asotea* when he was away at school. Unfortunately I got a few bumps in the process, so I lost interest before I really learned to balance myself. I finally gave up using *Tio* Gli's pair of roller skates, and I do not think he ever found out who had been using one of his prized possessions.

As expected, our interests changed over time as we progressed from slingshots and yo-yos to girls. Hence, that bicycle ride to Sarrat in the dark of the night. I did eventually graduate from apprenticeship when, later, the girls *Tio* Gli and I courted were sisters. That was when I was in high school and *Tio* Gli was in Normal School earning a teaching certificate. Times had changed, but I continued to emulate *Tio* Gli, for he had skills very much admired by members of the opposite sex. He danced gracefully, had a powerful singing voice, and played the piano well. So, in a sense I did not really stop being an apprentice to him, since I wanted to learn those same skills. Sad to say, my attempts to imitate *Tio* Gli's singing never amounted to anything I would care to remember, although I did eventually learn how to dance and play the piano.

I think *Tio* Gli was interested in body-building, too, for his older brother, *Tio* Deriong, had a lot of body-building magazines lying around. *Tio* Deriong was quite an *aficionado*; he spent some of his money for a magazine subscription, and was articulate about popular body-builders like Atlas, Sandow, McFadden, etc., and their techniques. There were a lot of barbells and dumbbells around . . . gathering dust I might add. But I think that was all that *Tio* Deriong could show for it. I do not remember him bulging with any muscles. Far from it! But such a home environment can be quite infectious, I am sure, and *Tio* Gli was soon into body-building. I do not think he developed any rippling muscles either, and finally contented himself with just being a theoretician of the art. But no amount of body-building could have protected them, anyway, for what was in store for them from the Japanese Military Police!

Tio Deriong's and *Tio* Gli's will and fortitude must have been tested to the limit when they were arrested and imprisoned by the Japanese Military Police towards the latter part of the Japanese occupation of Laoag. If I speculate on possible reasons for their incarceration, it could have been because (1) the Segundo farm in Surate, Dingras, was once a headquarters for the guerrillas under Captain Feliciano Madamba, (2) Madamba was recently married to

Auntie Anching, the sister of *Tio* Deriong, *Tio* Gli and my mother, (3) Madamba and Auntie Anching stayed at the Segundo house while Madamba was under house arrest after his surrender to the Japanese forces, (4) the guerrillas outside Laoag were becoming active again, probably encouraged by news via short-wave radio that the American forces were closing in on the Philippines, and (5) the arrest of a friend of the family who was tortured by the Japanese for information about guerrilla sympathizers. Very few came out alive after imprisonment by the Japanese Military Police, so you can imagine the fear in our family, not knowing the fate of *Tio* Deriong and *Tio* Gli. Prayers, waiting and more prayers were all the family could do.

Auntie Angeles, Mother's youngest sister, recalled that an officer of the Japanese Military Police who was an occasional guest to the Segundo house for dinner and *merienda* finally informed them that *Tio* Deriong and *Tio* Gli would be released soon. Imagine the muted jubilation and profound gratitude the family felt when my uncles were released, and finally came home physically unharmed. Only after they came home did we know how close they had come to not making it.

Tio Gli said that one night while they were still in captivity, all of the prisoners in the building were rounded up and loaded into the back of a truck. Before leaving for the river bank where executions were usually carried out, the same officer of the post, who had been a frequent beneficiary of *Lola* Leoncia's good cooking, came down to check arrangements before the truck's departure. It was then that the officer noticed *Tio* Deriong and *Tio* Gli were among the prisoners in the truck. After a short conversation between the officer and the soldiers, *Tio* Deriong and *Tio* Gli were ordered to get off the truck and escorted back to their cell. The truck then left, and came back later without the prisoners!

Tio Gli recalled later that the same Japanese officer who saved them from execution had sometimes brought ingredients for *Lola* Leoncia to cook, and readily stayed when invited for dinner. The Japanese officer admitted that he did not like garrison food. Being a graduate of culinary arts, I am sure *Lola* did wonders in her kitchen, which kept the Japanese officer coming back for more! When he was at the Segundo house, the officer, who spoke English, talked about his family and showed pictures of his wife and children, obviously missing them very much. When the Japanese forces in Ilocos Norte were ready to leave the province, the same officer paid his last visit to the Segundo House. He advised the Segundo family to leave for the countryside in case there was fighting in town. When informed that there were Japanese check points on the way out and that civilians were not allowed to leave, he prepared a note for them to show to the Japanese guards at these checkpoints. At that time, the rest of the Segundo family, who were still in town, did leave and waited at their farm for the transition between the departure of the Japanese from the town of Laoag and the arrival of the Filipino guerrillas. We often wondered whatever happened to that kind-hearted Japanese officer who saved *Tio* Gli and *Tio* Deriong.

Lest I give the impression that our interests were limited to matters of the flesh, such as homemade toys, bodybuilding, girls and more girls, *Tio* Gli and I did move on to more abstract matters. After World War II, *Tio* Gli stayed with us in our apartment at Lealtad in Manila when he attended Far Eastern University as a student of history. I recall discussions, after dinner, when he would expound on some of his interpretations of issues in historiography, citing some of his favorite historians like Agoncillo, Zafra or Zaide. As a student of the Social Sciences myself, these were occasions for lively debates, which I enjoyed. We were sometimes joined by "Vic Tom" (short for Vicente Tomas) who was a law student at that time. He was a bright young man who was Dad's hardworking assistant when we were still in Solsona during the war years. He followed us to Manila and was then living with us in Lealtad while attending law school.

Tio Gli and I became dedicated educators in our respective professional specializations. We eventually found the girls of our dreams; *Tio* Gli met Auntie Alice Dayandante of Albay, and I met Judith Elzinga of Michigan. Each of us settled into new lives in new locations and, fortunately, we can still look back and enjoy a lot of happy memories.

Home Away From Home

Anticipating the trip back home for Thanksgiving and Christmas vacations was understandably a happy time for most of the residents of the East Quadrangle dormitory at the University of Michigan. I was a resident of "East Quad," Strauss House, during my first academic year in Ann Arbor (1954–55). It was nice to be a part of that spirited group. Unlike some of the other foreign students, I had a "home" in Chicago where I could visit for a pleasant vacation. My family in Chicago included my father's brothers and their respective families. There was Uncle Fort (Fortunato) and his wife, Aunt Venay (Venancia), and their children, my cousins Anita and Richard. Living with them was Uncle Larry (Hilarion), a bachelor. Uncle Johnny (Juanito) and his son, Ronnie, also lived in Chicago, but in a separate house. I always stayed with Uncle Fort and Aunt Venay. Since Uncle Fort, Aunt Venay and Uncle Larry worked during the day, it was not until dinnertime when they would all be home again. Dinner was usually followed by delightful stories and recollections about their early days as immigrants in America during the early 1920s.

Ronald Takaki's scholarly work "*Strangers From A Different Shore*" (revised, 1998), provides an interesting history of the early immigration and challenges encountered by Asian Americans. The mainland U.S. Filipino population, according to Takaki, was only 406 in 1910,

> ...including seventeen in Washington and 109 in Louisiana—the descendants of Spanish-speaking Filipinos known as 'Manilamen' who deserted Spanish galleons in the eighteenth century. By 1920, there were 5,603 Filipinos in the mainland. Ten years later, their numbers had multiplied almost nine times to 45,208. (Takaki, p. 315)

Racism and discrimination confronted early Asian immigrants to the United States and, according to Takaki, more so on the mainland than in Hawaii. On the mainland, "Filipinos competed with white laborers and became the targets of violent white working-class backlash." About 25% of the Filipinos on the mainland in 1930 were in the service industry (e.g., janitors, dishwashers, waiters, busboys), 9% worked in Alaskan territory salmon fisheries, and some 60% worked in agriculture. (Takaki, pp. 316–320)

It was in this environment that Uncles Fort, Larry, Damaso, and Johnny faced the challenges of employment in the United States in the 1920s and 30s. Since they were sons of landowners in the Philippines and could have been influenced, to some extent, by the prevailing attitude of some upper-class Filipinos who tended to look down on manual labor, it must have required considerable adjustment in their thinking to support themselves with service jobs and manual labor while going to school in the United States. But probably more shocking was the unexpected discrepancy between their textbook knowledge about the virtues of democracy, as taught by American teachers who came to the Philippines in the 1920s, and how minorities were actually treated in American society. The fact that they survived racial discrimination without losing their self-esteem, without abandoning their goal to raise a family properly, and that they persevered to complete their college educations, attest to their resourcefulness, resilience, fortitude and determination.

Their effort to survive did not blind them to the plight of less fortunate Filipinos in the Chicago area. In this connection, Cousin Richard recalls a bit of history in the following:

> Dad had a steady job with the Post Office, and Mom was a nurse at Cook County Hospital. Their jobs were not affected by the depression. When relatives and friends from the Philippines came to Chicago and could not get jobs or find a place to live, my father and mother would take them in, feed them, clothe them, and help them on their way financially whenever possible. You might say they were like one of the stations of the Underground Filipino Railway.

It is fair to say that early immigrants like Uncle Fort and Aunt Ven represented a generation of pioneers who paved the way for younger generations of Filipino immigrants after World War II. Subsequent immigrants from the Philippines came as professionals, technicians, and as university students. It is reasonable to assume that they probably had an easier time in the United States materially than those who came in the 1920s. I emphasize materially because I believe prejudice and discrimination toward racial minorities are still very much alive in the United States today.

The civil rights movement of the 1960s revived the debate on the Fourteenth Amendment of the U.S. Constitution in terms of the meaning of "due process" and "equal protection of the laws." But because those who are elected to public office under our political system realize they can perpetuate themselves in power by catering to pressure groups that have the resources, in terms of votes and money, the debate on civil rights has been framed as a bipolarized paradigm of Black and White. The effect of this has been to marginalize smaller minorities like Native Americans or Asian Americans. Thus, for racial minorities who are not part of this dichotomy, it continues to be more difficult to land a job and/or compete for promotions.

I recall one personal incident that represented the folly and shallowness of a bipolarized approach to inequality in American society. In the early 1970s, after a few years as a member of the faculty of Eastern Michigan University (EMU), there was an advertisement seeking applicants for an assistant to one of the vice-presidents of the institution. Before I formalized my application, I went to one of the secretaries to inquire how the applications were shaping up and to express my interest. The secretary, who was a friend, advised me that I should not bother applying since I was not "black enough." She confided that that was what the university was looking for. That the university was not above playing the game of "tokenism" was, of course, extremely disappointing to me. Although I was aware of the practice in general (I have assailed it in my lectures), it was still a rude awakening on a personal level.

That was over thirty years ago, but has the mentality changed? In 2002, I called one of my former colleagues in the Social Foundations program in the Teacher Education Department at EMU. I was recommending an applicant for the faculty position that I had just vacated when I retired. Impressed by the applicant's strong background in the Social Sciences, I suggested they should look at his credentials carefully. The response I got was "We would prefer a Black applicant." The applicant happened to be White! As it turned out, the credentials of the applicant I recommended were far superior to the other finalists (which included, I was told, an African-American and an Asian American), so it was not too difficult to agree on his selection for the job. The person hired has been, I understand, a very productive addition to the faculty.

I strongly believe it is a disservice to racial minorities if it appears that they are being hired mainly for the color they represent to serve a university's idea of political correctness. It takes away the minority applicant's dignity, pride and satisfaction that can come from the knowledge that one is being hired for what he/she can do. If we hired and promoted on the basis of ability instead of color, maybe we could get closer to the essence of the Fourteenth Amendment as it was intended. I am sure that would also help to remove the inclination some people have to fawn shamelessly over selected minorities in social gatherings to dramatize their "commitment to diversity" while other minorities, who do not have political and economic leverage, are still fair game to their racist venom and hypocrisy.

On the other hand, it is equally important that all minorities do not capitalize on the fact that certain segments of the American population have been exploited and victimized in different ways. To capitalize on misfortunes of the past and expect handouts under the mantle of minority status, to my mind, is equally reprehensible. Maybe a thoroughly reformed system of education from pre-school to the university, including easier access, financially, to higher education, can provide better preparation for all citizens to compete on a "level playing field." That would also minimize "band-aid" palliatives that are extended to students who are already applying for higher education. Token remedies extended to applicants for college or university admission are a bit late indeed for reforms that really matter for a good education, human dignity and self-esteem.

Aunt Ven's experience continues to amaze me. It must have been even more challenging in the 1920s for a woman, considering that even today women are still demanding equality in the workplace. In spite of obstacles, Aunt Ven was a nurse and so she was recognized as a professional in Hawaii and later in Chicago. Aunt Ven and Uncle Fort were also active civic leaders, since they found time to participate in various Filipino organizations in Chicago. During the many times that I visited Chicago, she impressed me as lively, pragmatic and tough-minded. I have never forgotten what she said in one of our family after-dinner sessions: "If the opportunities are not there, Quirico, create them!"

Just as I have many wonderful cousins in the Philippines, I also have cousins Anita, Richard, and Ronnie (who has since passed away) in Chicago. Cousin Anita introduced me to pizza and to some of her girl friends. Like my brother Roly, Cousin Richard, who was then in junior high, was also interested in increasing the size of his biceps. Brother Roly and Cousin Richard would have been inspired, I suppose, by that popular advertisement of Charles Atlas about that skinny guy on the beach who was transformed into a muscular hunk! So the grunts and groans coming from Cousin Richard's room when he exercised were all too familiar to me.

My extended family in Chicago made sure that I was not lacking the essentials I needed as a graduate student at the University of Michigan. One evening Uncle Fort, Aunt Ven, Cousin Richard and I went to Sears Roebuck in Chicago where they bought me a windbreaker and a typewriter. The typewriter subsequently cranked out numerous term papers and eventually my doctoral dissertation. Uncle Larry made sure that I had more than my tropical clothes. He took me to Richman Brothers in Chicago. He said I should have a sport coat and gray flannel slacks "for more casual wear," a topcoat "for Michigan winters since winters will be quite different from your rainy season at home," and "something for special occasions." The last selection was a dark navy blue suit that, as intended, I used on many "special occasions." Little did I know it would be the suit I wore when Judy and I were married on June 11, 1955. This happy occasion was rendered more memorable by the fact that in the middle of the wedding ceremony I was suddenly struck by the thought that perhaps I had forgotten to remove the dry-cleaning tag, and that it might have been right there on my back for the whole congregation to see. At that moment, I began to sweat, not so much because of the seriousness of the commitment I was about to make, but because of the possible presence of a little laundry tag. The first thing I did after I was told to kiss the bride was to check the tag. Fortunately, there was nothing there.

More than the needed and appreciated material assistance provided by my uncles and aunt in Chicago was a sense of belonging and warmth engendered by the thought that I had a home away from home. Fortunately, I did not feel I was, if I may borrow the title of Takaki's book, a "stranger from a different shore."

Part II

I Remember Them Too

The following stories are additional recollections of growing up in Laoag, Ilocos Norte, Philippines. Although the passage of time has probably colored these memories, I like to believe the essence of the feelings they evoke—humor, excitement, respect, nostalgia, and happiness—is no less real to me now than when I experienced them.

"Snap Shots of the Neighborhood" describes a mixture of personalities and activities that were exciting from the perspective of a young boy, but were sometimes regarded with reservation by some of my elders. Thus, the family disciplinarian, Aunt Cristina, affectionately known to us as *Mama* Ti, tried, with good intentions, to shield us from the colorful language of *Baket* Sabel and from the influence of the neighborhood gamblers.

"The Lamplighter" is about the period before electricity came to Laoag. I did not know the lamplighter personally, but he was a part of my daily life as a young boy and, in a way, he represented the simple technology that characterized the culture of Laoag before electricity. He showed up every evening to light the kerosene street lamps, thus marking the end of another day. I remember how resourceful people provided light for their homes, and how this state of technology affected evening activities for the family.

"The Healers" recalls two unique and lovable personalities who were there when we needed them. They represented traditional folk medicine and stories from the spirit world; I always looked forward to seeing them for they provided exciting and playful images for my imagination. There is a third person recalled in the story, "The Vegetable Vendor." Although I never met the vegetable vendor who suggested a folk remedy for dysentery to *Lola* Leoncia, I have included a short account of that vendor because her remedy might have saved my life. Along with my gratitude to the vegetable vendor, I hope we continue to be open-minded about the possibilities of traditional medicine.

It is difficult to overemphasize the challenges and, certainly, frustrations that teachers face these days with pressures from increased cultural and ethnic diversity in the population, rapidly changing technology, and goals of education that are not always clearly articulated. If it is any consolation, effective teachers can make a difference in spite of seemingly overwhelming odds that beset them. In "Exceptional Teachers," I recall two sterling examples of dedicated, skillful and caring mentors whose legacy survives in the lives of former pupils.

"At the Farm" fondly recalls trips to the farm where the expected protocol between landlords and tenant farmers was disregarded by rambunctious boyhood adventures. Visits to the farm provided special memories about my boyhood in the province. It was a sparsely populated area, more quiet and more traditional than crowded, busy and noisy city settings like Manila.

Neighborhood Snapshots

A bird's eye view of Laoag in the 1930s would reveal a town laid out on a grid along the northern bank of the Laoag River with a population of about 40,000. The main thoroughfares were Rizal Street, which ran from east to west, and those which were known by their popular names, "Bacarra" (official name: General Segundo Avenue), "High School," and "Vintar" Roads, which ran from north to south. Smaller roads were situated between these main arteries.

There were sections of the town that had specialized functions. One was the town plaza. This was surrounded by government buildings, the Roman Catholic Church, the Aglipayan Church, and parts of the Laoag Central School complex. Another was the business section, along Rizal Street, in the central part of town. The public market was located here, and it was surrounded by Chinese retail stores. The business section was like a small Chinatown.

Residential neighborhoods surrounded these two main sections of Laoag. Houses were all single dwellings, a mixture of both large and small houses. Some were well-built with brick, cement and hardwood. Right next door might be simple bamboo and *nipa* huts. Thus, residential areas were inhabited by professionals, landowners, manual laborers, and others who did day-to-day labor when needed. This mixture of dwellings and residents of varying economic means could have been due, in part, to "squatting" on vacant lots by people from rural areas and by day laborers. Sometimes this arrangement resulted in a symbiotic relationship with the poorer segment providing labor for the wealthier residents of the neighborhood.

The diversity of socio-economic classes clustered in a neighborhood had its negative sides, too. There was sporadic gambling of all sorts: cock fighting, dice, *cara* (tossing a pair of coins and predicting the heads/tails combination), pool, etc. There was considerable quarreling in the open, and the language was usually colorful, which most people in the neighborhood found entertaining, except *Mama* Ti. She was Father's oldest sister, a school principal and the disciplinarian of the family. When she was home, she made sure that if there was gambling and/or quarreling in the immediate area, the children in our family were moved to the other side of the house, away from the disruption. In spite of these protective measures, it was easy to figure out who the "stars" were in some of these neighborhood activities. I mention some of them because, in spite of *Mam*a Ti's well-intentioned efforts to shield us from them, these people were a part of my social environment.

Baket Sabel

If ever there was a person who could out-swear the proverbial drunken sailor, it would have to be *Baket* Sabel. Some neighbors theorized that Sabel's propensity for colorful language was due to the mole situated near her mouth. Be that as it may, she provided entertainment for the whole neighborhood since the squabbles usually occurred late in the afternoon or at dinner time for most of us. Incidentally, that was just about the time of the day when there was an increase in consumption of the local brew, called *basi* (sugar cane wine).

Across the narrow gravel road from Uncle Vicente (brother of Father) and Auntie Onor's house was an open space surrounded by *nipa* huts, except for one portion that faced the street. *Baket* Sabel lived in one of those huts. The empty part of the lot was where the verbal combats usually took place. This was where it would progress after the initial salvos were hurled from the combatants' respective windows. The "stage", therefore, was conveniently situated for us to view from the porch of Uncle Vicente and Auntie Onor's house.

Baket Sabel was a formidable adversary. She was armed with a loud voice, an arsenal of invectives, and a rich vocabulary of four-letter words. These were skillfully applied to accusations of forbidden liaisons, real or imagined, and delivered with telling effect. In terms of audience rating, I am sure she was the main attraction of the neighborhood soap opera.

But my knowledge of *Baket* Sabel was not limited to a distant spectator-performer relationship. She later became a live-in maid of *Lola* Sabina. *Lola* had a *nipa* hut built on the family lot where the old Samonte house used to be. We visited *Lola* several times a day for she was practically next

***Baket* Sabel, the sharp-tongued protagonist**

door. Cousins Erning, Romeo and I slept in *Lola's nipa* hut and, later, so did *Baket* Sabel! I was just thirteen years old then, and I was apprehensive about being under the same roof with the fearsome Sabel. I would look at her surreptitiously when she wasn't looking. But I should have known better. Among all the maids in the Samonte household, she turned out to be the most soft-spoken and polite, and hardly spoke unless spoken to. I gave up trying to figure out her transformation, which I thought was like Jekyll and Hyde, for she stayed on as a loyal helper until *Lola* Sabina passed away. Thus, for all my fears that *Baket* Sabel might uncoil if she was provoked, it never happened. I was not as lucky with the gamblers in the neighborhood.

The Gamblers

When *Mama* Ti was not around, Cousins Erning, Romeo and I would watch the gamblers exercise their fighting roosters, or see a game of pool, which was set under a fruit tree. We knew when *Mama* Ti was due home from school so we could estimate how much time we had to be with the gamblers. During one of these excursions, we overheard the men discussing lucky charms for winning. One of the things that caught my attention was the luck that a twin-tailed *aloti-it* (house lizard) could bring if preserved in coconut oil that was prepared on *Viernes Santo* (Good Friday)! Flashing before my eyes was a vision of a windfall if only I could catch a two-tailed *aloti-it* and preserve it in *Lola* Sabina's coconut oil. Never mind if the oil was not prepared on *Viernes Santo*. At any rate, I remembered that when we slept at *Lola* Sabinas's *nipa* hut, house lizards would be crawling on the ceiling, looking for bugs and moths flying around the light bulb. The lizards were a source of entertainment for us when Erning, Romeo and I got ready for the night to sleep on mats laid out on the bamboo floor. I observed that the lizards had some kind of a pecking order. The most aggressive one was closest to the single light bulb where the insects were flying. Other lizards tried their best to survive with whatever insects came their way further away from the bulb. After a few nights of watching closely for a two-tailed *aloti-it*, lo and behold, I found one at the periphery of the whole bunch!

A plan was set. It involved enlisting the help of Erning and Romeo with the understanding that we would share whatever we could get from the sale of this precious commodity. It took about five nights, but we finally caught it! It was indeed two-tailed, possibly the result of mutation. We put the poor creature in a little bottle with *Lola* Sabina's coconut oil. There it was, all bottled up and ready for delivery. I do not know if *Lola* Sabina ever wondered about her depleted coconut oil.

It was another week, however, before we could get to the fighting rooster folks and the *aloti-it* was beginning to smell. We brought our prized possession to the gamblers, but the transaction did not last long. The gamblers looked at the bottle and expressed amazement that there was indeed a two-tailed *aloti-it*. The bottle was passed from one gambler to another. Erning, Romeo and I looked at each other, feeling very pleased. However, one of the men made the mistake of opening the bottle and smelling it! It was not Chanel No.5, I can tell you that. That ended, right then and there, our vision of making big money. Erning, Romeo and I left quickly for fear of physical retaliation from the gamblers, who cursed us for the foul smelling *aloti-it*.

Given that our business venture failed, we consoled ourselves with the thought that there were other sources of entertainment and opportunities for us in the neighborhood. There was always *Lakay* Ponsit who could be considered the James Herriot of the neighborhood.

Lakay Ponsit

If asked to name the most impish-looking little man that I have ever known, I would name, without hesitation, the good-natured *Lakay* Ponsit (Old man Ponsit) from our neighborhood in Laoag. Thinking of him reminds me of his distinctly high-pitched laughter and the ever-present fighting rooster that he cradled affectionately on his arm. But I remember him even more for his unusual remedies for animals that people brought to him with a variety of ailments, such as skin abrasions or just plain skin-and-bones cases of malnutrition. Laoag was essentially a horse-and-buggy town in the 1930s. There were just a few families who had cars, so transportation was dependent on walking, bicycles, horse drawn *calesas*, *carromatas*, and bull carts. Travel within the town was mostly by the horse-drawn *calesa*. Those who cared about the welfare of their animals and required the services of a specially trained person, such as a veterinarian, were out of luck, however, for there was no veterinarian with a private practice in Laoag. The few people in town who had a degree in veterinary medicine were employed by the government in breeding stations.

Enter *Lakay* Ponsit and his remedies. He would look quietly at the wound on an animal. These small open wounds or skin abrasions could have been caused by any number of things, such as an improperly adjusted harness or the animal rubbing against a wall. He gave the appearance of a serious and thorough diagnosis, accompanied by an occasional shake of the head and mumblings which were incomprehensible to those of us who were watching him. The kids would remain respectfully quiet, as would the *cochero* (*calesa* driver), who probably felt confident that his horse was in good hands. After a bit of suspense, *Lakay* Ponsit would announce that he was glad the animal was brought to him "in time," without explaining why. Having watched this ritual of *Lakay* Ponsit a number of times, I knew what was coming next. He would retrieve a dusty wooden box, which contained an assortment of small cans, bottles, a coil of rope, rusty-looking wires, etc. From this arsenal he would retrieve the same familiar red Hills Brothers coffee can, that he now used as a container of axle grease. This was his standard remedy, notwithstanding the suspense created by *Lakay* Ponsit's histrionics, employed, no doubt, to impress the trusting *cochero*. This "ointment" was applied liberally to the wound of the animal. I never knew what the grease did to the healing process. At the very least, it probably kept flies out of the wound. I do not think *Lakay* Ponsit was ever sued for malpractice. I never saw his picture featured in the local newspaper called *Silaw* (Light). As always, when *Lakay* Ponsit was done, the *cochero* handed over his payment with the unmistakable look of a satisfied customer.

A horse with behavioral problems, such as having the nasty habit of backing up when it should be moving forward while pulling a *calesa*, or just being "lazy" (probably from malnutrition) was an entirely different matter. But *Lakay* Ponsit was ready for these cases, too. For a horse that kept backing up, the old wooden box would come out and he would retrieve some of the wire, which turned out to be barbed wire. The barbed wire was carefully tied across the shafts of the *calesa* right behind the horse, where it delivered pointed reminders to the poor animal

***Lakay* Ponsit, the neighborhood "Vet"**

that it was going the wrong way. After a few stubborn trials, the horse probably decided the prudent thing to do was to move forward, away from the location of the prickly barbed wire.

For a horse that appeared listless, probably from not being properly fed, he had a special remedy. *Lakay* Ponsit retrieved from his box a large-mouthed bottle that contained more axle grease, but with a difference. This grease was mixed with one of the hottest local varieties of small pepper that was aptly called *sili ti sairo* (pepper of the devil). This mixture was generously applied to the posterior of the animal, right on a spot just below the tail, where it was determined to inflict the maximum effect. As expected, the poor unsuspecting horse would suddenly become agitated while *Lakay* Ponsit beamed with delight at another "successful cure." A small bottle of the mixture, which I called "Ponsit Special," was handed to the *cochero*, at extra cost, with instructions to apply it in the "correct" location.

In a way, the mixing of socio-economic classes in our neighborhood reflected Laoag society at that time. I believe my exposure to it, in spite of *Mama* Ti's efforts to shield her nephews and nieces from the colorful language and the gambling, has not corrupted or diminished me. On the contrary, I hope that it has made me more aware of how others lived: their pleasures, hopes, pains, and frustrations. It was part of growing up, beyond the confines of my family background, and I am glad for it.

The Lamplighter

He held the bamboo ladder on his shoulder, and a *bay-on* (a grocery-sized bag made of woven palm leaves) with his other hand as he approached the lamppost on the street corner. Since the lamppost was just across the street from the Segundo house, I always looked forward to the lamp-lighter's ritual. He would carefully position the ladder against the ten-foot concrete post and ascend with his *bay-on*. The amount of kerosene left was checked, more was added as needed, the wick was adjusted, the glass chimney was carefully wiped clean, and the lamp was finally lighted. After he descended, he expertly assembled his gear and moved on to the next lamppost, which was a couple of blocks away.

This time of the evening was also accompanied by a spectacular air acrobatics show of sorts. What looked like a giant black ribbon expanding to about fifty feet wide would emerge from the *Tabacalera* warehouse, located behind the Segundo house. The black ribbon kept getting longer as it spiraled into the sky for about fifteen minutes, while the other end was still coming out of the warehouse. As if on cue, the ribbon would break into small pieces, dispersing like a black cloud over the town of Laoag. Sometimes I imagined with my young mind that the spectacle was a huge serpent that emerged from its lair at the signal of the Angelus under the cover of approaching darkness. The gigantic "serpent" was actually thousands of bats that roosted in the warehouse during the day, and came out at night to hunt for insects. To me, the lamplighter, the ringing of the Angelus, and the spiraling bats signaled the end of another day.

Early evening was another occasion for more family activities. The kitchen was usually a favorite gathering place while dinner was being prepared. The women talked about interesting events of the day while helping the maids with small chores, like peeling the vegetables or sorting the rice or dried mongo beans. This sorting ensured there were no pebbles masquerading as rice or beans.

In retrospect, it is easy to remember the simplicity of the technology that, in the early 1930s, supported our life in Laoag. For instance, without electricity in the homes, light was provided by a variety of simple and inexpensive contraptions. A pressurized Coleman lantern provided the brightest light, but this was used in only a few houses, and also during some local festivities. More common were different types of kerosene lamps that used a wick. I remember one of these lamps that had an ornate base, a translucent glass shade and a glass chimney that protected and magnified the flame. This was used at the center of the dining table, and was transferred to the coffee table when we moved to the living room. Another kerosene lamp, which was home-made, was a small bottle covered with a metal cap that had a small tube in the center through which the wick was inserted.

However, the use of kerosene lamps lasted only as long as fuel was available. Thus, during the war years, when petroleum was not available, we had to devise other sources of light to supplement the use of candles. Our interaction with our tenant farmers during the war taught us more basic skills of survival. They had long used suet as a source of fuel. A small chunk of suet on a clay dish with a piece of fabric rolled and inserted to serve as a wick gave a nice light, one just as bright as the kerosene lamps. The tenant farmers also introduced us to the use of *saleng*, the heart of the pine tree which was cut into little strips that burned continuously. The farmers would fill an old clay pot or can with sand. Then they stuck a piece or two of the *saleng* into the pot or can. It burned like a candle. The supply of *saleng* came from the mountains where pine trees grew, and *saleng* cuttings were brought down by farmers who regularly trekked to the mountains, either to attend to their slash-and-burn agriculture or to gather firewood.

If there was a wind-up phonograph, a piano, a harp, guitar or ukulcle, those would have been the main sources of entertainment for the evening. For the kids, the excitement of listening to folk tales or ghost stories was enhanced when narrated in the dim light of the fire from the wooden stove while dinner was being prepared. Try telling a good story to small kids around the campfire or even by candle light, they will probably remember it for a long time!

The Healers

Ina Dora

Wrinkled, toothless and slightly bent over, *Ina* Dora (Mother Dora) was one of the residents in *Lolo* Segundo's *maguey* farm west of Laoag. She lived in an isolated section of the farm with her daughter, Anneng. Other members of the household included Anneng's son, Amor, who was in his teens, and Anneng's daughter, Lourdes, who was under ten. Anneng's husband was in Hawaii as a farm worker. *Ina* Dora was kind, witty and had a sense of humor. The Segundos were fond of her. She was always proper and respectful to *Lolo* and *Lola* Segundo, who were her landlords, but she did not hesitate to tease my parents, aunts and uncles, for she remembered them well as children. With amusement in her expressive eyes, she would ask how I was doing in school and whether I was behaving. I sometimes thought of her as a grandmother. Her *nipa* hut was the Segundo's favorite place for weekend visits at that particular farm. When we visited her, she could always be counted on to cook *dinengdeng nga manok* (boiled chicken with leafy vegetable), which she did very well.

Ina Dora was also a storyteller. She liked to tell us about the time when she was gathering herbs by herself late one afternoon in an isolated section of the farm, away from the gravel road. She was surprised, she claimed, by two unusually small women who suddenly appeared out of nowhere. She would indicate to us, with her hand, that the women were barely three feet tall. *Ina* Dora would imitate the tiny voice of one of them who asked *"Makigangat kami man basit, Maring."* ("Can we please have a light, *Comadre.*") "I was so scared," she recalled, "but I handed them my tobacco from which they lighted theirs. I looked the other way briefly, and they were gone just like that." This story illustrated *Ina* Dora interacting with a world that she believed in, a world inhabited by many spirits. The *aswang* (half human and half animal) could inflict bodily harm, the *mangmangkik* (which inhabit big trees) could do all kinds of mischief such as causing your hair to fall out if you maliciously threw stones at the tree, the *mangkokolam* (witch) that could concoct a powerful brew to make you sick, the *sinan padi*, a priest-like apparition that could only bring bad luck, and the *sinan Castila* (like a Spaniard), a white spirit that could change its size, move like a light, and then vanish right before your eyes. Her strong belief in her spirit world seemed to enhance her reputation as a healer among the farmers in the countryside.

One afternoon a barefoot woman with a shawl over her head showed up at *Ina* Dora's hut. She carried a small bundle wrapped in a knotted scarf. She inquired, in a hardly audible voice, whether *Ina* Dora was home. I ran to the kitchen of the *nipa* hut to tell *Ina* Dora about the visitor. She came out and greeted the woman who, from their greeting, I believed was a stranger to *Ina* Dora. After an explanation of the reason for the visit, *Ina* Dora invited the visitor to the kitchen of her *nipa* hut. This part of the house, probably no more than eight by twelve feet, contained nothing more than a small one-pot clay stove in a corner on the bamboo floor, a *malabi* (large red clay pot for water), two *banga* (black clay pots for cooking), a few odds and ends like ladles made of wood, and large coconut shells for plates. There were two or three *ikamen* (sleeping mats) rolled and stored standing in another corner. These mats, of various sizes for one or two persons, would be spread on the floor at night for sleeping. The kitchen was used as a sleeping area for *Ina* Dora and her extended family when we were visiting her for the weekend. My family slept on sleeping mats in another part of the *nipa* hut when we visited her. The bamboo slats for the floor were probably about one centimeter apart, convenient for cleaning, and efficient for ventilation. Over the years, the bamboo floor acquired a nice brownish patina from use and constant cleaning.

Ina Dora gestured to the woman to sit down, that would have been understood to mean "squat on the floor." Being a small boy of six or seven at that time, *Ina* Dora did not mind me hanging around, so I took my place on the floor

***Ina* Dora's remedy**

and listened. The visiting woman explained softly and slowly that her young daughter had suddenly developed spots all over her body, and while it did not seem to diminish her desire to play outside with other kids, the little girl complained about the spots being itchy once in a while. *Ina* Dora was quiet, a picture of concentration as she listened. She finally stood up and got a small bamboo basket from the corner. She brought it over to where we were sitting and rummaged through it. She took out a bottle of ink, a chicken wing feather, and a sheet of lined paper, similar to what we used in grade one for our writing exercises. Quietly we watched as she carefully opened the ink bottle, dipped the soft tip of the feather, and started drawing spots on the paper. She did not do it haphazardly, mind you, as she paused and seemed to ponder where the next spot should go. Satisfied that she had the right placements and alignments, she drew a circle around them as if to capture and control the power of the ink spots. After staring at the paper for a while, she folded it twice, and instructed the woman to hang the paper somewhere inside the house. As the spots on the paper faded, so would the spots on the girl. *Ina* Dora did not say how long this would take. The woman received the folded paper gratefully, carefully wrapped it in a handkerchief, and tucked it inside her blouse. She then opened the bundle she had with her, offered *Ina* Dora about half a dozen fresh eggs, and a few leaves of tobacco. She thanked *Ina* Dora, bowed slightly and left. I looked at *Ina* Dora with awe as she put her eggs and tobacco away.

Lakay **Siling**

It was *siesta* time and most of the adults would be asleep for an hour or so, a practice dictated by the heat of the dry season. Jose, Eli, and Rodolfo, three brothers from the squatters' area near the Segundo house, and I thought it was the right time to climb the guava tree in the Albornoz's backyard. The tree was now heavy with its ripe fruits, which were not too yellow. We stayed away from the overly ripe yellow fruits; over-ripe guavas are likely to have a lot of little things inside that wriggle like the snakes on Medusa's head! After scaling the bamboo fence, we quietly climbed the tree and started eating the deliciously ripe and aromatic guavas. We filled our pockets and the insides of

***Baket* Perpetua and the guava-eating kids**

our shirts. In our enthusiasm, we forgot all caution and began to chatter like excited monkeys who had just come upon a rich harvest.

Jose sounded the alarm. "She is coming!" The three brothers scampered down and ran away from *Baket* Perpetua Albornoz, who burst out of her house shouting invectives at us as she waved her broom. I was in the process of extending my reach to pluck a beautiful guava and was momentarily distracted by the commotion. I had to make a quick decision between getting down from the tree to get away from *Baket* Perpetua, who was now getting closer, or snatching one last fruit before making my escape. I chose the latter, lost my balance and fell to the ground. Unfortunately, I landed on my left arm. I got up quickly and noticed my arm had a funny dog-legged shape to it, starting at my left elbow. I quickly pounded it with my right hand and it clicked back into position. Luckily the old woman hobbled a bit so I got away with nearly all my guavas before she got to the base of the tree. Meanwhile Jose, Eli and Rodolfo were already on the other side of the fence, crouching and watching my narrow escape unfold before their eyes. To them, that close encounter with the likes of *Baket* Perpetua was the stuff that made leaders and heroes of men. Never mind that Jose and I were just eight years old, and Eli and Rodolfo were even younger.

That night I was not my usual alert and attentive self at the dinner table. I ate a little bit using just my right hand which, I was told later, my father noticed. When Father was helping me into my pajamas, he nudged my left arm on purpose. I cried out in pain. That was when Mother and Father had a closer look at my left arm, which was already swollen. After my recounting the events that led to my fall from the tree, one of the houseboys was sent to fetch *Lakay* Siling, the masseur who came whenever someone at the house suffered a minor sprain or dislocation. In a matter of twenty minutes or so, *Lakay* Siling, barefoot and dressed in homespun shirt and three quarter length trousers, showed up with his coconut oil, which had been "prepared on good Friday."

The rest of the family—*Lolo* Nicolas, *Lola* Leoncia, Father, Mother, Tio Gli, Auntie Angeles—and some of the maids, stood around my bed as they watched *Lakay* Siling approach me quietly with a somewhat set smile on his face. I thought his smile was calculated to convey his coolness and composure under such an emergency situation. He had what we might consider today a "good bedside manner." He applied some of the "Good Friday coconut oil" to his palms, touched my elbow gently, and passed his fingers over the swelling. Everyone in the room was quiet. He cupped my elbow with one hand, and very carefully tested the motion of my forearm, which made me utter a little expression of pain. He then announced to the family gathered around that he did not think there was a fracture. This broke the silence, followed by a stern reprimand from Mother and *Lola* about the need for me to mend my ways. Father was quiet. The maids enjoyed the guavas after Mother asked them to empty my pockets before taking my discarded clothes for the *lavandera* (laundry woman) to wash.

The following day Father's brother, Uncle Damaso, who was a physician, came to the house. He checked my arm, and confirmed *Lakay* Siling's diagnosis: no broken bones. Uncle Damaso took me to the Mission Hospital in Laoag so that *Tata* Sayas, one of the medical assistants, could put on a proper sling. I liked the sling because I got a lot attention from the neighborhood kids. Jose, Eli, and Rodolfo liked to tell the story about how it happened because they "were there."

The summer vacation was coming to a close and I was hoping my arm would still be in a sling when I got back to school. I thought of all the attention I would get, and how the story of my brave encounter with Baket Perpetua would be retold several times. But I had no such luck. By the time the school year opened, my arm was fully mended and I no longer needed the sling. I entered grade two without any fanfare.

The Vegetable Vendor

Because houses in Laoag in the early 1930s were not yet connected to the town's first electric plant (which was still under construction), I can remember a dimly lit kitchen at the Segundo house, faintly illuminated by a wood burning stove and a flickering candle. One evening, it must have been a somewhat subdued family sitting around the work-table. Our physician, Dr. Brilliantes, had just left the house. He had informed Mother, Father, *Lolo* Nicolas and *Lola* Leoncia that he had done all he could for me. I was of pre-school age, stricken with dysentery and, according to Mother, badly dehydrated and getting weaker with each passing day.

The morning after Dr. Brillantes' visit to our house, *Lola* Leoncia went to the public market, as she did every day, to buy vegetables and meat or fish for the day. Without electricity and, consequently, no refrigeration, it was necessary to purchase vegetables and meat every day. Given her frequent trips to market, *Lola* got to know some vendors better than others. Mother recalled that, when I had dysentery, some of the vendors regularly inquired as to how I was coming along. It was in one of those exchanges that *Lola* Leoncia informed the vegetable vendor what Dr. Brillantes had said during his most recent visit to the house. The concerned vendor suggested a folk remedy for dysentery to

Lola. The bark of the *lumboy* tree should be boiled, and the water was to be used for an enema. I guess when people are desperate enough, they are more inclined to try unconventional remedies to deal with their illnesses. *Lola* Leoncia had always been very attentive to any sick member of the family, and because she was attending to her only (at that time) grandson, she was probably even more concerned than ever. According to Mother, *Lola* immediately assembled what the vegetable vendor had suggested, prepared the material and administered the enema. Mother recalled: "After the foulest thing had come out as a result of the enema, you seemed to retain the broth and *segget* (the water that thickens when cooking rice) that we gave you. You began to regain your strength after that."

As a lay person, I cannot say for sure if there was a cause-and-effect relationship between the *lumboy* enema and my recovery. Looking back, I have been curious to find out what medicinal properties the *lumboy* tree might have that could have saved my life. The tree grows from between twenty and sixty feet tall. It is believed to have been introduced to the Philippines from India. Its fruit is about the size of a large olive and is eaten fresh. The *lumboy* trees were favorite climbing trees for kids during the summer when they were heavy with fruit, but a source of headaches to parents, for the fruit usually stained our clothes with deep purple. And it was difficult to deny that one had been climbing a *lumboy* tree, its fruit also stained the lips and tongue for all to see. According to Doreen Fernandez's book on fruits of the Philippines, some parts of the *lumboy* tree do have medicinal and industrial uses, including "bark *decoction* (which) is given internally for dysentery." (Fernandez, 29)

From the experience I had with *lumboy* and my bout with dysentery, I hope I always remember not to easily dismiss folk remedies. We are told that the great Dr. Albert Schweitzer learned to work with local medicine men while he was in Africa. I suppose he realized that if he could show his patients that he could work cooperatively with the traditional medicine men in whom his patients believed, it could also facilitate a more trusting relationship between Dr. Schweitzer and his patients. It is also encouraging that research in modern medicine now includes interest in acupuncture as well as in traditional herbal remedies.

I never had any difficulty accepting the value of some other remedies like sucking on raw ginger to help cure laryngitis or to "warm up the vocal cords" before a night of singing or serenading. Much to my embarrassment, however, I do remember that raw ginger did not always keep my voice from cracking (*agkiak* in Ilocano) when it was changing in adolescence, especially when I was the designated singer for a serenade. Pouring vinegar on fresh small cuts, which gave a bit of a sting, seemed to work in preventing infection. I did not know what tobacco did to a wound until one day, I saw a playmate, one of the kids at our farm, apply a piece of tobacco to his knee, which he had accidentally cut while chopping firewood. It had a little swelling for a few days, but his wound soon healed. Applying a freshly cut tomato or cucumber seemed to help relieve a minor burn. I modified that procedure once when I had an accident in Swaziland.

One day in Swaziland, I started to fry my dinner. I accidentally bumped the handle of the pan and catapulted the heated oil on to most of the back of my right hand. I immediately opened the refrigerator and pressed my hand against the wall of the freezer compartment while I brought out a tray of ice cubes with my left hand. With both hands, I quickly emptied the ice cubes in a bowl, added some water and promptly immersed my right hand in the ice water. I kept it that way for a few hours while I ate, read the papers and so on. I can say that I did not get any blisters whatsoever from that accident. The skin was slightly reddish, but no blisters.

I tended to be skeptical, however, about the practice in the working class neighborhood in Manila, where the older boys would circumcise the younger boys in some empty house or apartment. The kid who was being circumcised was asked to chew a wad of guava leaves. After the foreskin was cut, the chewed leaves were applied generously on the cut! I can say that when we all went back several days later to the "operating room" at an empty apartment to observe the removal of the bandage, I remember the penis of the youngster to be reddish and a little bit swollen. That seemed to be of no concern to the "surgeon." The boy who had been circumcised seemed to be all right after another few days, and was soon proudly swaggering in the neighborhood like a little man! Referring once again to the informative book of Fernandez, *Fruits of the Philippines*, she notes that guava leaves "crushed or chewed, are a toothache remedy, and in the traditional way of circumcision, are chewed by the subject to distract him from the pain, and then spat on the wound as astringent and disinfectant." (Fernandez, 15)

While it is easier to be open-minded about some traditional folk remedies that seem reasonable enough, it is more difficult in situations that border on superstition. I remember a number of times when I would notice banana leaves covering the window of a *nipa* hut in the villages outside Laoag. I was told the banana leaves were intended to protect the mother and her newborn from evil spirits. I have not yet found a credible reference to the practice of a neighbor who was suffering from a large goiter. She kept leeches in a bottle and regularly placed them on her neck to draw blood! In the case of a man bitten by a snake, my sympathy went to the chicken that was cut open, while it was still alive, and pressed against the snake bite. It was supposed to draw the poison out! The chicken ended up in the cooking pot. While the man bitten by the snake survived, we never knew whether the snake that bit him was poisonous or not.

Once, outside Manila, I was on a field trip with other students in a graduate class in Sociology at the University of the Philippines. When it was time for us to leave, there was a bit of apprehension on the part of the villagers. We were told that some of us had played with the local children and that we had "touched" them. We were puzzled and concerned that we might have inadvertently done something the villagers perceived as a breach of acceptable behavior. To our relief, all they wanted us to do was to make the sign of the cross on the children's foreheads so that, according to the villagers, we did not "take the children's spirit away with us!" Out of respect, we gladly took turns marking the kids on the forehead as the villagers demanded, and then we left with their hearty good-byes.

In spite of the challenges and difficulties lay people have in assessing folk remedies, I am forever grateful to that vegetable vendor who suggested a cure for dysentery to *Lola* Leoncia, and I am equally thankful that *Lola* Leoncia kept an open mind in trying it.

Discussing political and economic issues with Father after lunch.

Family picture with Father and Mother (front), L to R (back) the author, sisters Astrid, Amy, Francia and brother Roly.

With Uncle Damaso Samonte (*Tio* Papa) feeding the turkeys in the Samonte garden. c. 1932.

***Lola* Sabina with some of the younger grandchildren. c. 1960.**

Cindy (my second daughter) visiting *Mama* Ti and *Tio* Papa in Laoag, Ilocos Norte, Philippines. c. 1985.

Exceptional Teachers

***Manong* Ted**

The ugliness of war seemed to fade as the beautiful strains of various musical selections, such as *Hatinggabi* by Molina, *Tango* by Albeniz, *Meditation from Thais* by Messenet, or *Sonata in E minor* by Mozart, filled the air of the quiet neighborhood. At a time of night when I would lazily reminisce about the passing of another day and drowsiness would begin to set in, I always looked forward to the sound of the violin of *Manong* Ted Ruiz, who lived across the street from our house. He was a music teacher who worked tirelessly during the day teaching many children from the neighborhood and other parts of town how to play the violin. Still, he found time in the evening to play his violin, probably to relax, and we welcomed his renditions of beautiful pieces as the neighborhood gradually settled in for another night.

During the war, our lives were disrupted and children did not have much to do. But *Manong* Ted's music lessons focused on something beautiful for the young people and for others in town. When he arranged musical scores for his band, he made sure that even the youngest member of his many students had a part, even if it was just open strings with the violin! What a beautiful sound they produced when they finally played all together. His students would perform their "concerts" in town. These were usually well attended by proud families, as well as one or two Japanese officers who always dressed up for the occasion! The concerts brought people together, providing civility and some degree of refinement during the war years in Laoag. Ultimately, they provided some relief from the war that tended to brutalize our lives.

Manong Ted, as he was affectionately called, was an exceptional teacher and a wonderful human being. I cannot overemphasize the joy his music brought to our community, not to mention the special serenades I heard before I went to sleep. As a teacher, he was a master of his subject, and he was very effective in sharing his knowledge with his students. Even the slower pupils seemed to get as much of his attention as those who were more talented. He made learning fun, yet he never sacrificed discipline.

His two-story house and garden was like a little conservatory of music. The *sala*, dining room and porch were usually occupied with students either taking their music lessons or practicing. In the garden, the fruit trees provided shade for other students, who were rehearsing. All of these activities were made possible by the highly motivated students who practiced on their own, and by the older students who helped tutor the beginners. There were no discipline problems, no drugs to pacify students, and no drop-outs here. There were motivated students, supportive parents and a talented caring teacher. There were no air-conditioned rooms in the house, but the shade from the guava and *atis* trees was good enough, and having students in the *sala*, porch, and dining room did not even interfere with *Manang* Upeng's cooking and housekeeping.

I liked to hang around the house of *Manong* Ted and his wife, *Manang* Upeng. His younger brothers-in-law, who were my playmates, lived with them as extended family. I always enjoyed watching the students taking their lessons, with the older ones assisting the young beginners, and watching other related activities as they prepared for a concert. I was particularly envious when all the pupils dressed up for a community event.

Manong Ted probably assumed that I was also interested in music, since I was at their house a lot. One day he asked me if I had a violin. I said I did not have one. He must have given it some thought because a few days later he told me he had a small "banjo guitar," and he would be glad to teach me some chords. After giving me a few lessons, he assigned my friend Maring, his brother-in-law who was also a violin student, to play some pieces that I could accompany with my chords on the guitar. After a few rehearsals, *Manong* Ted told us "You two can now go caroling together."

Those who played musical instruments during Christmas usually received money from the families that they serenaded. Those who sang without instrumental accompaniment only got *tupig*, a traditional Christmas candy made of gelatinous rice flour mixed with coconut milk and sugar, wrapped in banana leaves and roasted slowly over charcoal. When the aroma of roasting *tupig* filled the air, it was an unmistakable reminder that the Christmas holiday season had begun. That was a memorable and happy Christmas for me. I learned to play a musical instrument, and earned some money, too. It did not matter that Maring and I could play only two songs; we moved from one house to another and collected our monetary gifts.

Mr. Baptista

Mr. Nicolas Baptista was my science teacher in high school. I have often asked myself why he impressed me as such an exceptional teacher. He knew his subject well, but that is just part of good teaching. He had a way of presenting science as a part of the larger picture of human events, not as isolated experiments to be memorized for tests. As one of the early Filipino returnees from the United States, he was able to weave some of his varied and interesting experiences into our lessons. He had worked in the fisheries in Alaska, in the farms of California and in helping lay out railroad tracks in the western United States. Aside from his ability to connect the lessons to everyday living, he constantly emphasized the importance of learning to be decent human beings along with our science education. I remember how frequently he used the word "dependability." To him it was not enough to be a skilled technician; it was just as important to be a good and dependable person. His science class attempted to reach the "whole person," as the jargon goes in colleges today. I hope he connected with other students as well as he did with me.

On one of my visits to Laoag, I was so pleased to have had a chance meeting with him at a social event. I introduced my wife, Judy, to him. But in the middle of a noisy dance hall, it was hardly the place to carry on a good conversation. I told myself that when I next got back to Laoag, I would certainly make it a point to visit him. My trips to the Philippines were so infrequent that when I did return to Laoag, a visit to Mr. Baptista was at the top of my list. Sadly, his daughter, a former classmate of mine, told me that he had passed away. If it is any consolation, I think good teachers live on in the legacy they leave behind with those who have been influenced in a positive way.

Manong Ted and Mr. Baptista live on in my memory as exceptional teachers who had skill, dedication and patience. They effectively shared, in a very caring way, their belief that we need to be responsible and decent human beings, and that this would serve as a foundation to become a musician, a scientist, a politician or whatever we wanted to be. Their teachings have resonated with me over the years as a teacher as well as a human being. I hope I have been able to share *Manong* Ted's and Mr. Baptista's philosophy, even in a small way, with the thousands of students I have taught as a college professor. It is a legacy that I also hope my grandson, and members of his generation, can appreciate as a part of their education in an increasingly complex world.

At the Farm

When I was still in elementary school, I would not have been able to think of anything more exciting than going to the farm with *Lolo* Nicolas Segundo. It was a part of his day every afternoon to go to the farm west of Laoag. It was only an hour away by our horse-drawn *caratela*. As a busy lawyer, going to the farm was his way of getting away for some fresh air and exercise. When he said "Junior, do you want to come?" it meant that I could climb some fruit trees (if they were in season) and slide down the sand dunes all the way to the river at the edge of our farm. Best of all was when he called out to the farm boys, Mariano and his older brother Cadio, who were both about my age. He would tell them "Help Junior get what he wants." For Mariano and Cadio this meant being released from farm chores to play with me. Aside from climbing the fruit trees that might have been in season, like guava, mango, *sirguelas*, or *caimito*, the best part for me was when they cut a special kind of bamboo called *bayog*. This had thick sides, a thin hole, maybe about the circumference of a pencil, and it was especially suitable for making popguns. I would get three or four nodes, one for myself and the rest for trading with the other kids in town. Mariano and Cadio made popguns for themselves, too. The other choice activity was looking for a *gosgosilat* shrub (another reference called it "*bolbolding*") which had symmetrical y-shaped branches that were strong and just right for making slingshots. I usually got three or four of those for more trading in town. When I went to the farm, it was also a chance for Mariano and Cadio to make their slingshots. I would bring extra scraps of leather, which I had gotten at the shoemaker's shop in town, and some good rubber from a piece of an inner tube. I shared these materials with them since they helped get the special bamboo and the *gosgosilat* for the slingshots. As twilight approached, *Lolo* would have the horse ready for the return trip to town. With all the fresh air and exercise, and with my treasured bamboo and slingshot frames in hand, I usually fell asleep before we got back to town. It was another special day indeed with *Lolo* Nicolas, and with Mariano and Cadio.

Another exciting activity at the farm occurred during the *abal-abal* season, which was a time for harvesting the June bug-like insects that came out of the ground at twilight before the rainy season. The farm came alive with activity and good fun as both older folks and children ran in the field to chase and catch as many *aba-abal* as possible. There were special techniques for catching the bugs. One method was to catch a female bug, if you knew how to distinguish it from the males. One would hold the female by its legs, and as it continued to flutter its wings, it attracted a lot of male bugs. We then quickly picked off the amorous males from the female bug and put them in a basket. This exciting and playful process lasted until the sun began to set. Landlords, tenants, grandparents, parents, and children would have a festive time together. The "harvest" would then be roasted, fried or steamed, to be eaten as a local delicacy.

The outbreak of the war and the invasion by the Japanese Army brought about the relocation of millions of people to places of relative safety in the countryside. This made it necessary for my family to move to the farm and live with our tenant farmers over an extended period of

Cooling off with *carabaos* at the farm

time. I evacuated with my father's family, so I spent part of the war at the Samonte farm (different from the Segundo farm which I visited in the afternoons with *Lolo* Nicolas Segundo). I had also visited the Samonte farm regularly before the war, usually during rice harvest time. My memories of the Samonte farm are equally as enjoyable as those I have of the Segundo farm.

Living with our tenant farmers for about four years during the war, starting when I was thirteen years old, gave me an opportunity to know them better. The tenant farmers' children at the Samonte farm became my friends too, and we shared a lot of memorable times together. We had great fun swimming in the small stream at the farm when they watered and bathed their *carabaos* (water buffalos) at midday, when it was too hot for either man or beast to work in the fields. I might add that the back of a *carabao* made a fairly handy jumping board. Being carefree and rambunctious, we hardly paid any attention to what the *carabaos* must have been adding to the water as they placidly wallowed, seeking refuge from the tropical sun.

While at the farm, there were other adventures. One of them stands out in my mind. I had quite a scare with a *beclat* (constrictor snake) that was coiled on a trunk where I was about to place my foot. At approximately two yards above ground, I was busy picking *gawed* (beetle leaves) that the old folks liked to mix with beetle nut for chewing. Noticing the colorful pattern on the *beclat* (my foot was barely a yard away), I dropped to the ground in a flash. I do not remember the sensation of ever touching the ground, even in my bare feet, but I

Close-call with a *beclat*

ran home as fast as I could. When I told the old farmers about the constrictor, its location, and how big I thought it was, they reminded me that I was lucky I was still alive to tell them about it. They warned me not go to the woods by myself again, especially when the sun was about to set!

Not long after I finished high school in 1948, I visited the Samonte farm again. I noticed then that the sons of our tenant farmers, whose companionship and adventures I had shared in the woods with our slingshots, swimming in the water hole, and sleeping outdoors to guard the pile of newly harvested rice, related to me differently. They treated me as the son of their landlord, observing the social distance and respect they thought constituted proper behavior towards me. This puzzled me and it was indeed a disappointment for the adventures I shared with them were treasured memories from my boyhood.

For decades after 1948 when I left for the University of the Philippines in Manila, I no longer had the time to visit either the Segundo or Samonte farm. But when I returned to the Philippines for Father's funeral in 1998, I made an effort to visit the Segundo farm, which was closer to Laoag since that was all the time I could spare. That was the place that *Lolo* Segundo and I used to visit in the afternoons in his horse-drawn *caratela* when I was in elementary school. My sister, Astrid, and her husband, Lito, were kind enough to drive me over.

It was late afternoon when we got there. I looked around trying to reconstruct what I could remember of the place from fifty years ago. Instead of one *nipa* hut, there were now about half a dozen houses clustered in the same area. I asked one of the women if they knew any of the people who used to live there. They told me that some of them were still around, that they were the children and grandchildren of Mariano! Remember Mariano? I asked if he was at home, not wanting to ask whether he was still alive. I maintained my composure, but I felt a bit anxious as I waited for their answer. "He is in the field somewhere. He should be coming home soon." I thanked them, and walked by myself to an open field where we used to catch *abal-abal*. I stood by myself and watched the valley as I welcomed a flood of happy memories. It was almost sunset, and I could still make out farmers in the distance, bringing their animals in from the fields.

In a short while, I noticed a solitary figure on the trail coming slowly up the hill, bent over with a load of firewood on his shoulder. One of the kids came to where I was standing to let me know that Mariano was coming. I thanked her, and I waited. About ten meters away from me, Mariano stopped, and slowly lowered his load. He was barefoot and stood by his load as he looked at me. After a moment of silence, he asked softly, "Dinyor?" (Junior). We were about the same age, but years of living a hard life had made him look even shorter, slightly stooped and wrinkled, very different from the young boy I remembered. I felt sad and I reflected on the inequities that attended our different lives. I walked over and put an arm on his shoulders. I am sure it was an awkward moment for him for I represented the landlord and he was a tenant farmer. The landlord-tenant relationship was formal. Formalities were not important to me, and I never expected them from our tenant farmers. I was just pleased and thankful to see an old friend again.

Part III

Growing Up

The following are experiences that stand out in my mind. Some are remembered fondly and some still make me shudder when I realize what dire consequences I, as well as others, might have encountered. The "Walk Home From School" was, by itself, a good excuse for going to school. The different local artisans, their concentration, their little tools, their dexterity, and their finished products—be it a repaired old watch, an article of clothing, a balanced bicycle wheel, a pair of shoes, a saddle, or even a coffin—were endlessly fascinating. I guess that little boy's curiosity has not left me, thank goodness, for even now I am just as drawn to people who produce interesting and beautiful things with their hands. Whenever I visited Chinatown in London in the 1980s and 90s, I always made it a point to pass by a particular restaurant which had its kitchen right next to the sidewalk, separated by only a large glass window. It was just as fascinating to me, as it had been many decades ago in Laoag, to watch the Chinese cook go about his business with the skillful use of his cleaver, the quick movements from chopping block to wok, and the inviting presentation once he had assembled everything in what seemed like a very short time.

"The Other Side of the Road" provided adventure and opportunities to know kids who were raised under different circumstances from those I was familiar with at home. How I envied some of the things they would brag about, some real and others imagined I am sure. Fortunately, members of my family were quite supportive of my effort to expand my circle of playmates in the neighborhood. It opened up new perspectives for me, and it might even have added some hardness, toughness and stubbornness in my determination to survive.

As I describe in "Close Calls," there were situations, partly of my own making, that exposed me to some risks. In retrospect, I would concede that responsible adult supervision is essential for young kids as they grow up in an increasingly complicated and, sometimes, more dangerous environment. I was lucky to survive some of the foolish activities I was involved in, and am thankful I am still around to write about them, as a warning rather than boasting about them.

"Getting Acquainted" recounts some of my clumsy excursions into "urban society." Going to the University of the Philippines exposed me to a different stratum of society with its frills, rituals and social pecking order. It was indeed very different from the refreshingly less pretentious lives of the neighborhood kids from the "school of hard knocks" back home.

I have included "To Da Woods" under this section partly because my decision to stay in the United States, after completing my graduate studies at the University of Michigan, represented a drastic change in my life. In a sense, my adjustment to a different culture also included a lot of "growing up."

"Barong by Pierre Cardin" recalls how I eventually became more critical of indiscriminate importation of material goods and ideas from other countries, especially from former colonial powers. I hasten to add that while I do believe a country's heritage is enriched partly by its contact with other cultures, the process of assimilation and integration should be selective. This view represents a refinement in my thinking. It is a change that probably came about as a result two things. One was the internal struggle to define who I was culturally whenever I was confronted, while in the United States, with obstacles to employment or promotion. The other was a greater awareness on my part of the marginalization of some ethnic minorities.

Walk Home from School

It is probably fair to say that it takes more than skill and patience for teachers to stimulate and maintain the interest and focus of elementary school children when dealing with such subjects as arithmetic or language arts. As a student, I certainly did my share of daydreaming. The start of the rainy season, for example, meant opportunities to build toy boats to float on the inundated drainage canals. The long summer vacation promised all kinds of non-school activities like climbing fruit trees and going to the Laoag River for a swim and a picnic. The Christmas holiday season was ushered in with the unmistakable aroma of baking *tupig* and *bibingka*! I was susceptible to the siren call of these seasonal events.

When in the classroom, I also looked forward to my five-block walk home from the Laoag Central Elementary School by way of Rizal Street, which was the main thoroughfare of Laoag, through the central business district. It was paved with asphalt wide enough for two cars, but the traffic consisted mainly of a few *calesas* (horse-drawn carts), *carison* (bull carts), bicycles, and pedestrians. Within this central business district, it would not have been unusual to see stray dogs, goats, and even a sow and its piglets scavenging along the street. On weekends, bull carts parked under the *acacia* trees, and the barefoot farmers fed their animals while waiting for their women, who would be at the public market selling firewood, vegetables, clay pots or stoves that they brought from the farms. These vendors would in turn buy some necessities from the *ka Sanglayan* (Chinese section), necessities like *sabon ti Sanglay* (Chinese soap) for washing clothes, matches, kerosene, salt, etc. to take back to the farm village.

The street through the business district was lined on both sides with assorted retail stores. These were housed mostly in old one-story buildings made of brick, concrete or wood, with galvanized iron roofs that extended over a cement sidewalk. Each store had large doors that provided ample view of the goods on display for sale.

It was along Rizal Street that I viewed a variety of small shops and artisans located between the stores. There was, for example, that glum and forbidding watch repair man who had, to my young imagination, the appearance of "Limahong," the legendary Chinese pirate who terrorized the inhabitants along the Philippine coastline. The tailor shop was always a beehive of activity, with experts marking and cutting expensive-looking cloth, and the sound of treadle sewing machines that seemed to harmonize with the lively chatter and laughter of the tailors. In contrast was the quiet concentration of the shoemaker with his evenly placed hand stitches. The more rugged-looking saddle makers cut smoothly into large pieces of cow hide with their sharp knives while they talked about interesting matches of fighting roosters at the *gallera* (a small enclosed arena for cock fighting). Their ever-present fighting cocks were tethered to pegs around the premises.

The *panaderia* (bakery) was also a favorite of mine with its display of assorted cookies, breads and cakes. The wonderful smell of freshly baked bread, especially during *merienda* time, lingered as I moved on reluctantly to the next shop. The dexterity of the Chinese noodle maker and the contraptions he had for kneading a large mound of dough were always interesting, even if I could only see him through the bamboo fence.

The liquor dealer, with the beautiful but strange wife, usually stirred my imagination, which was fed by the rumor around town regarding the manner in which he was supposed to have concocted a special cocktail to win the hand of a former starlet. An entirely different marital combination was the elderly vulcanizing shop owner, with his young wife who always seemed to be breast-feeding a baby, and what seemed like a dozen noisy children running around in the small shop.

To my young mind the barber shop was a place where important issues of the town were discussed. I did not understand much of what they discussed but I thought they were interesting, nonetheless, for the manner in which discourse was carried on with spirit and laughter. They spiced up their discussions occasionally with gossip about local personalities which I found to be even more interesting.

Baket Molang (Old woman Molang), who can probably be characterized as the Julia Child of the neighborhood, had a stand where she sold "*adobo*" (spiced pork and/or chicken), *longanisa* (sausage) and *dinardaraan* (pork cooked in pork blood with spices). Customers usually included workers on their way home, who might want to bring dinner home, and some who might stop by for a little *pulutan* (snack). The attraction for me was not so much what she was selling, but the hope that one day I would get lucky and witness ashes falling from her big *dinubla* (rolled tobacco usually bigger than a cigar) into the cups of soup that she ladled to sell to unsuspecting customers. Fortunately for her customers, I never saw it happen (much to my chagrin).

The most intriguing shopkeepers were the coffin makers, who made me wonder what types of people would go into the business of measuring dead people and building coffins for them! My interest in coffin makers took a downturn once when several older boys asked me if I knew how coffin makers stayed in business! As if sharing a well-guarded secret, one of them whispered that coffin makers kidnapped kids who were hanging around, especially when the coffin business was slow! They looked at each other as they savored my wide-eyed reaction. On the way home I kept telling myself that this could not be true. But just to be safe, I started walking on the other side of the street until I convinced myself that it was probably another one of their jokes. Still, it was with some apprehension that I resumed my walk and my usual stop at the coffin makers' shop. This time I was on high alert. I eyed them sharply, wondering if what I had heard could be true as I watched the lame carpenter shuffle around the shop. Like a bolt of lighting, I got up and ran when the carpenter, after picking up a scrap of wood, hollered to his companion, "Here's another one!" Without looking back, I ran as fast as I could all the way home.

The intriguing sights, colorful verbal expressions (which I dared not repeat at home), assorted aromas, textures and skills were far more stimulating to me than any lessons my elementary teachers provided in the classroom! In retrospect, maybe there is something valid to the view that for education to be meaningful, interesting and effective, it should also reflect appropriately the life and environment students are familiar with. In this connection, I wonder whether American teachers are adequately prepared to discuss analytically the varied and important issues confronting the population of the United States that is becoming increasingly diversified racially and culturally.

Other Side of the Road

By the time I was giving my third lecture on desegregation of public schools in the United States, I began to notice the same expression on the faces of a quarter of my students, reactions I had noticed in previous semesters when I covered the same topic. It was a combination of indifference and boredom. These students were undergraduates, predominantly white, and enrolled in my class called "Schools in a Multicultural Society," a required course for prospective teachers for Michigan public schools. With a mixed feeling of anger, frustration and disbelief, I struggled through the lecture. I later shared this experience with colleagues who were teaching different sections of the same course. I felt a little relief when they confirmed the same reactions from some of their students when they discussed related topics like poverty, racial minorities, and problems of achieving equality in the schools. My frustration continued, however, because I thought it was incredible that these prospective teachers, who would be certified in just two years, could not see the value of learning and understanding the important challenge of inequity in public education.

I decided to confront the problem head on. Emphasizing the view that the face of America is changing and many of their future pupils will not look and think like them, I asked my white student teachers if that was of any concern to them as prospective teachers. Would they want to know who their students are, how they think, how they learn, what they believe in and why? Did those questions matter at all or, because they would be the teachers, would they simply impose their knowledge and values upon their pupils?

I pursued this by requiring the students to write a five-page paper describing the influences in their elementary and high schools years that might have shaped their attitudes towards people of other races. Analysis of their papers revealed a lot of interesting information about my students: many came from small communities where there were no racial minorities, some had parents who had discouraged them from interacting with African Americans, and some were actually exposed at home to negative remarks about non-whites. Eyeopeners for them included the church they attended, meeting new friends in high school, going to college where exposure to other races in the classroom and dormitories was unavoidable, and travel. A few believed or hoped they would end up teaching in a predominantly white school anyway.

The experiences described by my students were consistent with the type of students attracted by Eastern Michigan University, mostly from the surrounding counties and a few students from Ohio. It was not surprising to me, therefore, when I read a letter to the editor of the *Ann Arbor News* (January 10, 2002) from a teacher in Chelsea (Michigan) public schools who complained about the attitude of her students and the Chelsea Board of Education toward Martin Luther King Jr. She wrote in part:

> Close to 20 years ago, while teaching at Beach Middle School in Chelsea, I was shocked to find fewer than 50 percent of my eighth grade students knew about Martin Luther King Jr. and his role as a nonviolent leader in the civil rights movement. At that time I attempted to organize a school observance day, but was met with staff resistance. Next I approached the Chelsea Board of Education. I shared my concern about our students' lack of knowledge about King and suggested a district-wide observance. The response I received was that Martin Luther King and his non-violent leadership in the civil rights movement was not relevant to Chelsea students.

In a way, the response to the teacher in Chelsea was essentially the same as what I got when I called, in the early 1980s, the principal of an Ann Arbor elementary school to inquire if they had any course that taught anything about multiculturalism. Answering somewhat impulsively and sounding a bit irritated, the principal said "We do not need such a course since all our students are white!" When I countered by pointing out that that should be a good reason for having such a course, she responded with a *non sequitur* "We have that, too." End of conversation.

* * *

While my experience growing up did not involve the issue of race, for I came from a racially homogeneous population, there was differentiation based on socio-economic status. For example, there was distance between social classes in terms of playmates, who went beyond elementary grades, who attended college, and who got married to whom. As far as my choice of playmates was concerned, I was fortunate to have parents who encouraged me to play with all the kids in the neighborhood. The one restriction they had was that we were forbidden to go into any household that had someone who was known to have tuberculosis. This was another situation when Mother would use the code word "spreading" to warn me about communicable and infectious diseases.

Aside from play situations, my early interest in earning money resulted in additional exposure to a variety of kids. With the various schemes that I hatched, I had lots of opportunities to play and interact with children from other neighborhoods. One of my projects when I was in grade school was to be a bootblack on weekends. With a little "capital," advanced by aunts and uncles after convincing them I could make money by shining shoes, I made a triangular-shaped wooden box. Then I collected used toothbrushes for applying dye, and purchased shoe polish, brown and black dyes, and bigger brushes for buffing shoes.

I soon learned that the other bootblacks each had different sections of downtown claimed as their territory, and the bigger boys expected other bootblacks to respect these boundaries. The amount to be charged, according to the type of shoes, was also strictly observed. A single color low cut shoe for adults was three *centavos*. To charge less would surely get around very quickly, and one would soon be cold-shouldered and endlessly harassed for it. For black-white or brown-white combination shoes, one could charge from seven to ten *centavos* according to how intricate the pattern. The most expensive and difficult job was a shiny white pair of shoes. That required a higher level of skill. That would have cost the customer up to twenty-five *centavos*, if the bootblack did not ruin it! For a pair of simple white suede (*gamosa*) shoes, I charged ten centavos.

Another enterprise I undertook, dealt with peanuts. I did not sell peanuts, but I observed that the vendors used newspapers to wrap roasted or boiled peanuts. They charged one *centavo* for roasted or boiled peanuts packaged in a small cone-shaped container fashioned from the newspapers. I collected the out-dated copies of *Manila Daily Bulletin* from my relatives, and also my *Lolo* Nicolas' *La Vanguardia*. I made money selling the papers by the kilo. I kept my customers satisfied, and made sure I charged less than any of my competitors.

A kind of a barter system flourished at our elementary school as kids exchanged one item for another. Examples include exchanging a live hermit crab for a pencil, a marble for a crayon, colorful bottle tops for a piece of candy, a top for a slingshot, etc. I soon became an active participant in this barter system and I searched for things at home that the other kids might want. *Lolo* Nicolas used quinine regularly which came from the *farmacia* in a small tubular bottle about two centimeters in diameter and six centimeters long. He discarded the empty bottles. I realized that if I removed the labels and filled them with water, the bottles made good magnifying glasses! Not knowing whether this item would sell, I brought them to school anyway and made a big sales pitch about the exciting things I was observing. The other kids soon got curious, and I was ready for them. I had ten bottles in my school bag just in case!

Other items to trade were pieces of leather, which I got outside of a small shoe factory where the workers would throw away remnants. They were just scraps of shoe leather but they were well suited as material for slingshots. This was my hottest item indeed, especially for the boys whose slingshots had just been confiscated by the principal of the school. You would think I was in collusion with the authorities, for it was my *Mama* Ti who was the principal. If she only knew about my business on the side!

I believe my work experiences also made me more appreciative of the value of getting a college education. As I got older, I worked as an orderly at a United States airbase. This was after the Japanese occupation ended but before the high school reopened. I was also an assistant to a surveyor for the Public Works Department when the municipal government prepared the drainage canals before the rainy season. And I worked as a painter for a government housing project during the summer while I was in college. These jobs provided extra income for school, but it did not take me long to realize how painfully monotonous they were. It was also a rather gut-wrenching realization that many of my co-workers depended upon such employment for their livelihood, and that they did not have the alternatives I would have, provided I stayed in school.

After reflecting on my own background and going through the short essays of my students, I believe their indifference towards class discussions of cultural diversity, poverty, racial discrimination, etc., resulted partly from of their relatively sheltered life, from parents who discouraged them from having anything to do with racial minorities, and partly from public schools that did not incorporate information about multiculturalism and inequalities in our society. From my perspective, I was thankful that my parents, aunts and uncles were very supportive of my efforts to explore my social environment through play and work experiences. It had its risks, but I strongly believe it increased my awareness of social and economic opportunities and inequities in our town, and hardened my determination to do well in school.

While I was fortunate enough to have had a diverse experience in terms of playing, working and going to school with children from other social classes, it was still a challenge for me to figure out what I needed to do for my students, who appeared indifferent to class discussions about problems of ethnic identity, inequities in education, and other people less fortunate than they were. In an effort to stimulate the students' interest in the ethnic diversity of American society, I realized I had to go beyond understanding the influences that shaped their attitudes. From the papers that they had submitted to me, I gathered that at least some of the students would be willing to break away from their parochial upbringing. With that as an incentive, I explored ways to make the issue and discussion of inequities in education more interesting to my students.

I started with the assumption that students are not usually keen about reading textbooks on social foundations of education that, according to them, they had often found dry and uninteresting. I also had to recognize that instructors, too, sometimes found the textbooks in teacher education dull and uninspiring. Accordingly, I wondered if it would make a difference if I changed the reading materials from conventional textbooks to more popular literature, such as novels, biographies, etc., which people seem more inclined to read. My quest led to the development of a course which I offered the following year. I called it "Understanding Ethnic Identity and Cultural Diversity Through Literature." Although offered as a graduate course, some colleagues suggested that I should offer it as a 500-level course. This would allow undergraduate seniors to enroll with permission from the instructor. Thus, the first time I offered it as an experimental course, I had a mixture of undergraduate and graduate students.

To provide a framework for the analysis of the student-selected materials for individualized book reviews, the course started by looking at selected sociological, economic, legal and political perspectives. These would serve as a theoretical framework to help explain what was happening in their book selections—causes of alienation and how they were overcome or minimized, the role of people, institutions and events in facilitating cultural integration, and factors promoting understanding and pride in one's ethnic or racial identity. These guidelines for analysis were intended to keep the course from deteriorating into just a "reading for enjoyment" activity.

I am pleased to report that this was one of the few courses I had taught at the university level where students actually stayed after class to continue discussions, and brought additional books to class, on their own initiative, for possible addition to the thirty-five-page syllabus. Some students asked if they could review two books instead of just the one that each had selected as per course requirement. Needless to say, it was a highly satisfying course for the students and for me. From the more animated discussions in class and how some of the students volunteered to do extra readings and to present longer reports than required by the syllabus, it is reasonable to infer that the course stimulated the students towards a greater understanding of cultural diversity.

Another interesting development, which I did not anticipate, was the students' view that the format of the course had possibilities for the elementary grades, middle school and high school. The students thought that the application of the format of the course to the lower grade levels might encourage the students to read given the use of more interesting reading materials and, in the process, learn more about their society which is becoming increasingly diversified culturally and racially.

Close Calls

If I were of grade school age today growing up in the United States, I would probably be a prime candidate for *Ritalin*, its prescription possibly suggested by a teacher who does not have any medical training. (See *Time*, November 3, 2003 on "a medicated generation") I was a very active young boy who got into all sorts of mischief, both in school and out of school. I was a bit of an instigator, so I sometimes got other kids involved in my "escapades."

When I started a new grade in elementary school, the standard procedure was that *Mama* Ti, who was the school principal, would introduce me to my new teacher. She would give specific instructions that I was not to be given any special treatment. I suppose this implied that the usual application of the ruler stick to the posterior of an erring student applied to me. Teachers would assure *Mama* Ti not to worry, that every thing would be all right. I include the following events in my recollections only as examples of poor judgment on my part. I was supervised as much as any prudent and responsible family would have provided for their children. Unfortunately (for my parents), I had a way of undermining or circumventing adult supervision, a skill that came in handy later, when I wanted to outwit chaperons when I started dating in high school.

Some of my mischievous deeds were minor enough. When I was in grade one, I stuck a piece of gum on the hair of the only child of the school superintendent. Imagine the teacher's alarm when the little girl started crying. It was just an impulse on my part to stick the gum, but it got more tangled in her hair when I tried to remove it. In desperation, I thought of cutting off that part of her hair, (each one of us had a small pair of scissors for paper cutouts) but surely that would have made the situation worse.

Another episode involved my scattering salt, at the suggestion of the houseboy, Ciriaco, under the chairs of a couple who frequently visited our house and who usually showed up shortly before dinnertime. This always delayed mealtime for us and, more importantly for Ciriaco, it delayed his night out. The houseboy believed that salt under visitors' chairs would drive them away. What made it worse, however, was when Father and Mother noticed that I was under the visitors' chairs and asked me what in heaven's name was I doing! I innocently announced that Ciriaco asked me to put salt under the visitors' chairs! I was forgiven for that, but my elders were definitely less forgiving when I converted *Mama* Ti's favorite piece of furniture into a pool table! To her, it must have been convincing evidence that her efforts to shield us from the gamblers in the neighborhood were not very effective. Nonetheless, the wooden ruler that was applied with authority to my open palms was surely a painful reminder of the disadvantages of being the oldest nephew. Because I was the oldest among the nephews and nieces, I was supposed to be a role model of proper behavior. Instead I was usually presumed to be an instigator; that great legal tradition of presumption of innocence was forgotten. Consequently, cousins Erning and Romeo were spared the rod in this particular episode, even though they had participated in the conversion and use of the pool table.

In spite of what appeared to be a propensity for mischief, I must mention that I did not neglect my responsibilities in school. I was careful not to lose sight of that "balance." For example, when I was in grade two, I represented my elementary school in a declamation contest at the Laoag town fiesta, after a process of elimination that included contestants from the upper grades of the elementary school. I also participated in plays and folk dances in elementary school. While attending high school, I served as class president for the junior and senior classes, and I represented the province of Ilocos Norte as an athlete at the Inter-Provincial meet in Tuguegarao, Cagayan. My academic average in high school was high enough that I was exempted from the entrance examination for admission to the University of the Philippines. I later received a scholarship from the University of the Philippines to pursue graduate studies at the University of Michigan.

But there were other incidents, indeed, when I do have to admit *mea culpa*. These incidents were not trivial matters for, in each one of them, I could have lost my life. I am referring to two particular incidents, one in which I almost drowned in the Laoag River and one when I was almost electrocuted at the Laoag Plaza.

During the summer, the Laoag River was a silvery ribbon that flowed lazily towards the China Sea. It originated from the blue Cordillera mountain range in the east, and flowed past bamboo groves, small farms, a few villages, and an isolated *nipa* hut here and there. During the rainy season, it became the color of a chocolate milk shake that churned and frothed as it tumbled towards the sea. Although usually three to four times wider than normal during the rainy season, the river tended to be confined within the broad area of the sandy river bed.

The graceful Gilbert Bridge that crossed over the river, providing access to Laoag from the south, was a favorite strolling place for young people. It had two sidewalks from which to enjoy the misty Cordillera mountain range in the east or the colorful sunsets over the China Sea in the west. The Gilbert Bridge was built during the early part of the American occupation of the Philippines as part of the development of an economic infrastructure of the country. During summertime, on moonlit nights, the dry portion of the river-bed was a favorite place for children's games, like "capture the flag," and it was also a choice location for lovers out for an evening walk.

Sadly, the beauty of this river is now a mere memory, as it is practically dry during the summer and there are more ferocious and destructive floods during the rainy season.

This development may be attributed to unregulated logging and slash-and-burn agriculture in the mountains, activities which have been going on for decades. The increasing negligence of some provincial leaders and the abuse of the land by slash-and-burn farmers have finally caught up with the Laoag River. The younger generation may now be deprived of some of the activities that used to be provided by this beautiful setting.

My first near-drowning incident happened when I was in kindergarten, age six, at the Holy Ghost Academy, which was located right next to the Laoag River. Instead of going home right after classes were over for the day, another classmate and I decided to go to the river for a "short swim." By then, it was getting late in the day and the women who usually did their laundry on the river-bank were gone. There was one *cochero* near where we played; he was bathing his horse. The other boy jumped from behind me and pushed both of us into a drop-off. What followed was a desperate struggle for air as the other kid started to tighten his hold around me. Neither of us knew how to swim. After what seemed like an eternity, we found ourselves on the shore, exhausted and feeling bloated with water. Without the *cochero*, who noticed our struggle and who pulled us out of the water, I have no doubt what the outcome would have been.

By coincidence the *cochero* was formerly in the employ of my family so he recognized me. On his way home, he passed by our house to report the incident to my family. I received the worst beating in my life from *Lola* Leoncia, my

Near-drowing in the Laoag River

maternal grandmother, who used her leather slippers for emphasis.

In spite of that terrible beating, I thought it was safe enough, when I was in grade two, to go to the river again with "older" boys who knew how to swim. There were about eight or ten of us, and we did not know enough to have a system of keeping track of each other. With the help of the swimmers, we all crossed a narrow portion of the river, where it was probably about eight feet deep, to get to a sand bar about twenty feet from shore. We played in the water for an hour. Then, as it was time to go home, the others crossed the deeper part again. Since we were enjoying ourselves, it must have been easy for the older boys to overlook the whereabouts of the non-swimmers, such as me, when they started to return to shore. I followed behind without the help of the swimmers. I was soon under water in spite of my effort to stay afloat by kicking against the bottom of the river. I began to sink when I could no longer touch the sandy river bed to kick and to keep my head above water. Just then a stem of a banana plant floated over my head. I made a quick grab for it. With all the strength I could muster, I put my head above water and shouted "Help! Help!" Only then did the others, who were already getting dressed, realize that I was missing. The older boys promptly jumped into the water to rescue me. I was eight years old.

Local events, like a town fiesta, were occasions to decorate the town plaza to make it look festive. This usually included stringing up lights with frayed electric wires that were periodically retrieved from government warehouses. Like moths drawn to the light, children would congregate to play in brightly lit sections of the public plaza. It was in this setting that, while balancing myself on one of the railings, I lost my footing and quickly grabbed at the wire overhead to keep myself from falling. Unfortunately, it was a bare electric wire. I started to shake violently. Luckily, my fall to the ground separated me from the wire, but I continued to shake. I could not stand on my feet and my eyelids fluttered. I could make out that people were starting to crowd around me but they did not dare touch me. I do not know how long it took, but I finally stopped shaking while I was still lying on the ground. I sat there for a while. I was exhausted. A few people stayed but did not say anything.

What could they say? It was starting to get dark, the church bells rang for the Angelus, which was my usual reminder that it was time to go home. I slowly walked home, which was only a block away.

Father and Mother were busy dressing up for the public dance, to be held at the public tennis court, which was enclosed for the town fiesta. Without paying much attention to me, Mother told me to go to *Nana* Elisa's house to get fresh flowers for their corsages. I knocked on the door. *Nana* Elisa came out and as she guided me to her garden, she placed her hand on my head. She promptly asked me what I had done to my hair. The question surprised me, but I suspected that it might have been due to the incident with the electric wire. I responded quickly that we had been fooling around with my aunts' curling irons. I remember she mumbled, "Naughty boy!" With this added information, I made sure I stayed in the shadows when I got back to the house so my parents would not see me. I gave the flowers to the maid for delivery to Mother and Father. As soon as they left, I went to the mirror to see what *Nana* Elisa was asking about. To my surprise, I can say that my hair looked like the hair of Albert Einstein, as I remember seeing in pictures of the well-known scientist. Unfortunately, that was probably the only thing I had in common with that famous man as far as my head is concerned.

At any rate, I had to think quickly before Mother and Father returned from the dance. I went to the bathroom, filled a basin with water and soaked my head. I alternated this with vigorous combing. I do not know how long I repeated that process, but ultimately, it did the job. Mother and Father never knew they almost lost their son that evening. If I act overly cautious or protective today as a father and grandfather, it is these close calls that still evoke memories and make me shudder. Life is indeed beautiful and precious.

Family and friends seeing me off when I sailed from Manila for the United States. 1954.

Arrival in San Francisco, California, with other students from the Philippines. 1954.

Stop-over in Hong Kong on the way to the United States, 1954.

Judith Elzinga, 1954.

Serenading Judy, University of Michigan, 1954.

Spring term picnic, University of Michigan, 1955.

Judy's mother, Evelyn Elzinga.

Judy's father, Eugene Elzinga, M.D.

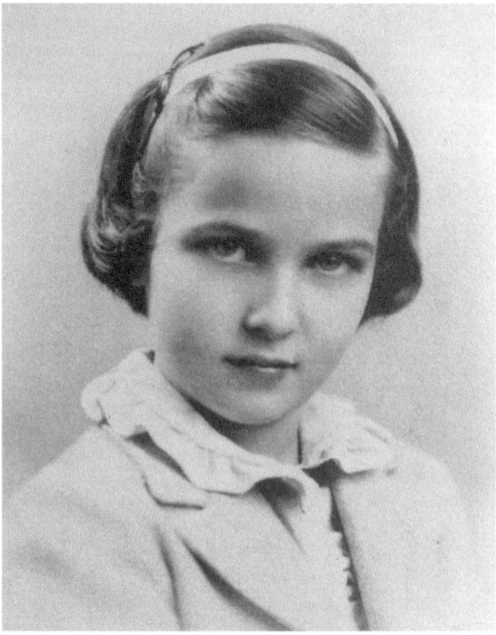

Young Judy.

Daughters Cristina and Cynthia in school uniform as grade school pupils in England.

Cristina with Grandma and Grandpa Elzinga. Marquette, Michigan.

Cristina and Cynthia with Grandpa Elzinga.

Fortunato Samonte (Uncle Fort) and Venancia Siazon Samonte (Aunt Ven) as early Filipino immigrants to the United states in the 1920s.

Getting Acquainted

"He is the nephew of ____." "He is the cousin of ___." So went the variety of opening lines that a friend of mine used whenever he introduced me to his "socialite" friends in Manila. It was a source of embarrassment to me, so I told him I preferred to be accepted for who I was, not because of my family connections. He assured me it was okay and not to worry. He added, "They probably won't pay much attention to us unless we do that." Being the son of a high-ranking officer in the Philippine Armed Forces, he circulated among a particular social class, and he thought he knew the protocol and symbolisms of social acceptance, at least in the group with which he was familiar. Much as I did not go for that, some of the girls he knew were extremely good-looking. So I told myself, "What the heck" and went along with this charade.

For my amusement, I reviewed this ritual of introduction, since various societies have different ways of pegging people within their social structure. In the 1950s,

Philippine society was relatively static in the sense that the same families seemed to dominate the economic, political and social settings. Thus, it was relatively easy for the educated segment of the urban population to recognize names of people who were usually in the news, especially those who were featured regularly on the "society page." Within this context, the process of introduction at a Filipino gathering when I was in college could have gone something like the following: If my family name happened to be similar to that of somebody important, the first question to me could very well be "Are you related to____?" My response could easily change the dynamics of the social interaction right then and there. If there was no family connection, but there was still some interest in me because of some mutual attraction, additional probing followed with questions about which high school and/or university I attended, whether I was a member of a fraternity and which one, and did I know so and so. From this line of questioning, it was quite clear that even if I was not a member of a "prominent" family, I should at least be acquainted with the "right" people. If satisfied with my credentials, I was then introduced to the other members of the "in" group.

If one had no blood relatives, close or distant, who might help boost one's social status, a little imagination might fix that. I was told of someone who liked to tell people that General Gregorio del Pilar, a historical figure during the Philippine-American war, was his "godfather." Never mind that Pilar had been killed in the late 1890s and would not have been around in the 1920s to be a "godfather" to anybody. I nonetheless wondered how del Pilar, long turned to dust, would have reacted to the fact that his extended family was still growing!

Coming to the United States with these experiences in social introductions required changes in my expectations. In large urban settings, money, professional achievement and/or race, in that order, appear to be more important, at least as initial measures of a person, than family name, unless the name is Ford, Rockefeller, or John Gotti. Some Filipinos residing in the United States have made adjustments, although at Filipino gatherings they may still use family name as a social booster or as a connector when meeting first generation immigrants. However, their children, who were born in the U.S., probably could not care less.

In the following observations about social introductions in a particular small town in the U.S., I cannot overemphasize the fact that my comments are drawn from my impressions as an "outsider" who has never felt fully integrated culturally and psychologically into that amorphous entity called "American society." From that perspective, these are recollections from limited exposures to and interactions with a small part of a highly diversified American culture. My comments should not be construed, therefore, as generalizations about a particular town or about other places in the United States. I leave the task of generalizations to social scientists and survey experts.

In Marquette, Michigan, my wife's birthplace, where I visit regularly it has been difficult for me to avoid forming some impressions about parts of the community and some of its people. In describing what might appear as relatively egalitarian in a very circumscribed setting, I am not unmindful of the existence of a stratified socio-economic structure in the larger community of Marquette based on type of employment, income, ethnicity and race. Finally, African Americans are just now appearing as residents in and around Marquette, a new experience for a politically conservative community. But I will not dwell on this level of abstraction. I will focus instead on face-to-face interactions with some people I have dealt with in Marquette.

While there is still some degree of name recognition for the "old families" when it comes to social introductions, one's inquiring about family relations seems to be more about connecting someone to a former classmate from elementary or high school. Thus, a plumber, an electrician or a carpenter, for example, coming to the house for work, upon learning that you grew up in town, is likely to spend time exchanging pleasantries and asking which grade school or high school you attended. This seems to be less for placing positions in the social pecking order, than to establish a possible link to some people you might know in common.

I remember the young man who replaced the fifty-year-old oil furnace in our cottage in Marquette. He kept us entertained with bits of information that he shared with us while he worked. We have enjoyed, for instance, reports of his "finds" in garage sales, such as old folding cameras and pocket watches, things he recently saw in an "Antiques Road Show" program. He told us of his sighting of a bald eagle near one of the shopping centers in Marquette, about the size of some of the brook trout he caught and more he could have gotten, had he not fallen asleep.

One day he asked if Judy's maiden name was Elzinga. When Judy confirmed that it was, it started another line of conversation: he mentioned that Judy's dad, an orthopedic surgeon, had mended a fracture the young man suffered when he was in grade school; and Judy's brother, Don, who is also an M.D. had been on call in the emergency room and removed a fishbone from his throat when he was a kid. He further related that his father and grandfather had installed the furnace at Judy's family house when it was built about sixty years ago. I find such chit-chat interesting and entertaining for it underscores the humane and appreciative connections some people seem to have with one another even from one generation to the next in this particular town, regardless of socio-economic status.

You may be wondering, given all the chatting, if the furnace technician was too distracted to do his work effectively. I would say his work was first class. The young technician represents those traditional workers who still take pride in the quality of the work they do. As a matter of fact, it amused me to watch him fix and wipe that old oil furnace, almost affectionately, when he would come over to clean it for another season. It always reminded me of Charlie Allnut, the character Humphrey Bogart played in the movie, *African Queen*, and how he cared for the old steam engine on his boat. Our furnace technician never got to the point, however, of having to kick our aging oil furnace to make it work. The old one was replaced with a "high tech" furnace before that ever happened.

Meeting the two burly iron ore miners sent over by the furnace technician to haul away the old heating unit was also an interesting experience. As they maneuvered the heavy old furnace out of the utility room, with barely an inch to spare through the narrow doorway, they still found time for small talk. They shared information about locations for good wild blueberry picking and brook trout fishing. On their way out, they casually asked if we liked blueberries or brook trout. We said that we did. One evening about a week later, there was a knock at our door. There were the two miners and the wife of one of them. They explained that they had been out fishing that day, and since their freezers were already full, they thought about giving us their "catch of the day." They had brought over about two dozen brook trout, already gutted and cleaned! But that was not all. The wife said she had found a good wild blueberry patch while the men were fishing, and she gave us two to three quarts that she had picked that day! Judy and I had tasty brook trout for dinner and Judy baked a delicious wild blueberry pie. It was an unforgettable evening, thanks to the thoughtfulness and generosity of those miners in the Upper Peninsula who dig for iron ore, an industry that is barely surviving.

Parenthetically, the rescue of the trapped miners in West Virginia in 2002 was a heart-warming story, an impressive application of technology and an encouraging faith in the human spirit demonstrated by those who labored to free their fellow workers. What a contrast to those overpaid financial and executive officers involved in the corporate scandals that have dominated the news lately. I like to believe that the two miners we met, and those involved in that rescue in West Virginia, are representative of their fellow-workers who labor hard to earn an honest living, face the dangers involved, and still find the time and disposition to be generous and to share what they have with other people. From this perspective, it nourishes my faith in the goodness of people. I hope their example, strength and patience will prevail over the greed and callousness that seems, unfortunately, to have infected our society.

I am sure the criteria for social position in the Philippines are changing and will continue to change. There are still awkward moments in social introductions, however, when one cannot keep track of who the right spouse might be. In the Philippines, one who is brazen enough to bring his mistress to a social function must be careful not to introduce the mistress as the wife. Equally distressing is my experience at social introductions in the United States when I was not informed ahead of time about somebody's second or third spouse. It is not always easy to keep up with the progression and identities of those who have had serial marriages. In spite of these first impressions, I hope we find the time and disposition to know each other better as individuals, to know who we are beyond the conventional criteria that society often uses to position us in the social pecking order, be it in Manila, Marquette, Ann Arbor or elsewhere.

Unfortunately, what sometimes passes as scholarly analysis of ethnic identity and/or behavior tends to treat cultures as monolithic, be it Asian-American, African-American, Hispanic-American or European-American. To that extent, individual differences are obscured, stereotypes are reinforced and we continue to regard each other from a distance. Face-to-face introductions and meetings do provide opportunities for knowing one another, if we do not let social conventions get in the way.

"To Da Woods"

After college, I had to make the very difficult decision of whether to remain in the United States or return to the Philippines. Staying in the United States after completing my graduate degree meant living away from my family, other close relatives, and friends I had known since I was in elementary school; giving up a promising position that was waiting for me at the University of the Philippines; abandoning all thoughts of eventually getting into Philippine politics, an ambition that I had cherished with strong passion since I was in high school. On the other hand, the attraction of staying in the United States included being in love with an attractive and bright student, Judith Elzinga, whom I had met at the University of Michigan. The challenge of overcoming obstacles to a successful career at an American university was appealing. It was difficult to ignore the possibility of better opportunities in higher education for my children, should I have a family of my own. And there was that remote chance that I could get involved in a United States foreign aid program for possible assignment in the Philippines.

The challenge of settling down in a "different culture" was never an issue with me. The use of the English language, the idea of democracy, and the "Protestant Ethic" (in terms of hard work to get ahead) were not alien to me. Similar values were pretty much a part of my upbringing and were emphasized by my family. Material conveniences in the United States were never an attraction for me since my life back home was, for me, adequate materially and certainly more leisurely. On a social level, the question that I did examine closely was the prospect of becoming a "second class citizen," given what I knew about treatment of racial or ethnic minorities in American society. It has been with a lot of effort that I have, in my mind, wrestled with that issue over the years, and I still continue to rationalize about it in order to be able to live with it.

On a more personal level, in terms of my relationship with Judy, my concerns were more cultural than racial. For instance, I considered our expectations in terms of gender roles, such as child rearing, housekeeping, and other aspects of the division of labor between a husband and wife. In this connection, it is fair to say that our respective families probably had more misgivings about the racial and cultural aspects of the prospective marriage than Judy and I did. On my side of the family, Mother reminded me that the marriage of Uncle Johnny, Father's younger brother, to an Italian-American in Chicago, had ended in divorce. She mentioned this in one of her letters, and never brought it up again. Father did not express any opinion on the matter. I guess we all face, at one time or another, important junctures in our journey through life. The decision to stay in the United States was indeed an important turning point for me. We make as good a decision as we are capable of making with the information available, and we move on with our lives.

Since one of the key factors that led to an important change in my life was being introduced to Judy, I should relate how this fateful meeting came about. In 1954–1955, I resided at the East Quadrangle dormitory of the University of Michigan during my first year as a graduate student in Ann Arbor. I had a single room at Strauss House. The other residents were mostly undergraduates, and they were friendly and relatively well-behaved. One Friday evening a couple of them dropped by my room to inquire if I had any plans for the evening. I told them I did not have any, and would probably stay in to work on my term paper. They informed me that they were going to a Psychology Club party in one of the apartments close by and they left the address, in case I changed my mind. By nine o'clock in the evening our floor was almost deserted, and I was getting tired with my schoolwork. I decided it might not be a bad idea to check out the party the boys had mentioned. I took a shower and changed into my party clothes.

As it turned out, the apartment address was only a few blocks away from the dormitory. I entered through the main door of the apartment and there was dance music

Meeting Judy for the first time

coming from a phonograph. In the dimly lit living room I could make out three couples dancing. A student came over to greet me and informed me that there was a keg of beer in the bathtub. I thanked her, and proceeded to the bathroom to get myself a glass of beer. My eyes finally adjusted to the light and I started to size up what the girls looked like. Not very promising, I thought. I sat on the stairs while I enjoyed my beer. Another fellow was sitting on the steps.

We exchanged small talk to the extent possible under the circumstances. It was then I noticed one of the girls who was dancing. She was dressed in red, and was attractive, but she also looked tall. Sizing up her height, I noticed she wore high-heeled shoes. I could not tell if the fellow she was dancing with was her boyfriend, but I concluded he looked a bit dilapidated. I approached them as soon as the music stopped. "Good evening," I greeted her. I continued "I'd like to dance with you if you take off your shoes!" It was a rather bold and unconventional approach and, frankly, I did not know what kind of response I would get. To my surprise, she said "Yes." Off with her shoes, and away we danced. Judy always hastens to explain that her lack of umbrage at such a "cheeky" approach was due to the fact that she had noticed me at a university sponsored dance two weeks prior to that night. Since then, she had hoped to meet me and so she determined that she would not let a "pair of silly high heels" interfere with this opportunity to become acquainted.

My standard procedure when I met a likeable young lady was to ask what academic field she studied, where she resided, and so on. And if she was willing to exchange phone numbers, that was encouragement indeed. Mother of surprises, Judy told me she was a resident of East Quadrangle, and so was I! "East Quad" was the only co-educational dormitory at the University of Michigan in 1954. It was divided into different "houses," most of which were men's residences, but two, securely locked at night, were for women. She was a resident of "Tyler house" while

I was at "Strauss house." To make a long story short, that was how Judy and I met. We were married in her hometown in Marquette on June 11, 1955!

I had become, through marriage, a member of another family, but was it going to be "home" for me? Getting to know Judy and the members of her family was one thing, but becoming a part of her family was another. Her father, mother, two brothers, and her Aunt Lorraine, who was her mother's sister, were all graduates of the University of Michigan, as were several of her father's sisters. But what appeared as an unusual family loyalty to the University of Michigan did not end there. Judy's sisters-in-law, Nettie Jean Blake, wife of Eugene, Jr., and Katherine Elizabeth Tanner, wife of Donald, were also UM graduates. I will leave to psychologists to ponder whether or not this family loyalty to the University of Michigan is some kind of aberration. At any rate, the fact that we were in this unusual circumstance together probably facilitated my integration into Judy's family.

Decades have passed since June 11, 1955. The Elzinga family has grown and so has mine. I have come to know a close-knit and caring extended family. Being at the table with Judy's family was a joyful and informative event, just as I recalled my experiences growing up with my family. For example, during conversations at the table with the Elzinga family, the dictionary was sometimes brought out to resolve the correct spelling of a word, a word's origin, a word's alternate meanings, etc. Except for cultural variations, the values Judy's family lived by, things like the belief in hard-work, the pursuit of excellence, the dedication to valued principles, a sense of responsibility to town and country, and being just and honorable when dealing with members of the family, as well as with the public, were essentially the same as those that were emphasized by my own family.

On more trivial matters of acculturation, I have learned to like an Upper Peninsula favorite, meat-potato-rutabaga filled pastries called *pasties* (pronounced 'pass teas' and not to be confused with the tiny attire of striptease dancers). It was even easier to develop a taste for thimbleberry jam, made from berries which family members picked along the road, and prepared at home. For some reason I have never acquired the same enthusiasm that Judy has for plain boiled and buttered rutabaga. I consistently resisted Judy's mom and Aunt Lorraine's efforts to teach me how to play bridge. I must add that I was amazed by what appeared to me to be an obsession with physical exercise, held by some members of Judy's family. Do not get me wrong about my attitude towards the benefits of physical activity. As a former varsity athlete in track and field and in baseball, with awards to show for it, I do not dispute the value of proper exercise. But I draw the line somewhere, especially after one Christmas vacation when I allowed myself to be persuaded to join Judy and her brothers, Gene and Don, to go snow shoeing to a place outside Marquette they called "Hogback." They outfitted me with what looked like a pair of old tennis racquets on my feet and off we went. After trudging for what seemed like an eternity in wet snow, my snowshoes were getting heavier. I wondered about the rationale of romantic

Snowshoeing on Hogback, Marquette, Michigan

instincts that had brought me to this predicament: namely walking aimlessly like a fool in what seemed like the Arctic Circle. As a result of this misadventure, I missed a good dinner of pork roast which my mother-in-law had waiting for us when we got in from that dreadful expedition. After soaking in the tub, I went to bed with the intention of resting a bit before dinner. While the aroma of that roast and homemade apple sauce drifted upstairs, I promptly fell asleep and did not wake up until breakfast time!

Even with each summer's arrival, I can say that the prospect of my being a more integrated family member, as far as exercise is concerned, has not improved any. Judy and her brothers and sisters-in-law continue their regular walks through the woods, in pursuit of that proverbial fountain of youth. Unfortunately, for me the arrival of summer also means blood-sucking mosquitoes, flies and ticks! So, no walks in the woods for me! I limit myself to enjoying, from a distance, a view of the woods and the lake from our deck with a cup of tea and a good book. I will just take my chances with premature aging if that is what awaits me! Isn't retirement wonderful?!

Now on to more agreeable topics, like those that appeal to my sweet tooth! Thimbleberry jam is one of my favorites, with just the right amount of tartness when made without too much sugar. Thimbleberries are, according to Bob Krum in his informative *The Great Lakes Berry Book*, (1996) "the same genus as raspberries and blackberries, but the plant looks like a maple bush. The large maple-like leaves are the size of saucers. The blossom is big enough to be a daisy." Krum also notes that the plant is not widespread in the Great Lakes region but is found in "Michigan's Upper Peninsula, the northern fourth of the lower peninsula, far northern Minnesota, southwestern Ontario and southern Manitoba. However, thimbleberry is widespread in the Rocky Mountain West and the Northwest."

Because it is not cultivated commercially, it is harvested only from roadside patches or along railroad tracks. Thimbleberry jam is therefore not available at regular grocery stores. It can be bought once in a while when an enterprising housewife might bottle some and sell it at a roadside table, at a garage sale or at a church or school bake sale. It also was offered as a prize during an evening's entertainment after a hearty dinner of authentic Upper Peninsula *pasties* at our "Paul Bunyan" night. The event was held annually at Eastern Michigan University for former residents of the Upper Peninsula employed by Eastern Michigan University. It was sponsored by the president of the university, a Scandinavian who had previously lived in Marquette, Michigan. A jar of thimbleberry jam was awarded to the person who could tell the best Scandinavian joke for the evening!

It is quite understandable, therefore, that *aficionados* of thimbleberry jam are secretive about their favorite locations for picking berries. They can give you the cold shoulder if you show up at their secret locations to pick thimbleberries! They will give you that "where-did-you-come-from" look. It's a silent treatment, as cold as the water of Lake Superior. On one of these occasions, Judy and I went to a place where we had spotted some berries earlier, near Wright Street just outside of Marquette. We were ready with our empty plastic milk bottles cut away on one side, to use as a receptacle for the berries we would pick. Upon arrival, an elderly man and woman were already at the location picking thimbleberries. They looked at Judy and me, but gave us none of the usual congenial Upper Peninsula friendly greeting. It's that thimbleberry thing again, I thought. I did notice, however, a mellowing in the expression of the woman after she took a second look at me. She must have figured I was a Native American and decided she should mind her manners or I might start invoking my "rights" under some old treaty. Thus, we silently picked our berries without any federal incidents!

Other experiences with mistaken identity have been a source of amusement for me. Once while out for a drive near Lake Michigamme, Judy and I decided to stop at an antique shop. After looking around the store, I asked the attendant if they had any old cranberry pickers. She seemed puzzled, so I explained that it is made of wood and looks like a rake with long crooked teeth attached to a box. They did not have any, she said. Then she added, "Your people eat a lot of cranberries, don't they?" Sensing another case of mistaken identity, I rose to the occasion by responding that we did consume a lot of cranberries. "How do you eat them?" she asked. I have to apologize to all concerned for this impulsive act of impersonation, but it was too good an opportunity to miss humoring the woman for her stereotypical comments. I went on to describe a fictitious concoction which I called "Mo-mash." Since she wanted to know more about it, I explained that it was a mixture of honey and berries during the summer, and a mixture of berries and snow during the winter. Mashed to perfection, it was, I exclaimed, "out of this world." Judy looked at me reproachfully, but she maintained her silence until we got back to the car. There were other incidents. Suffice to say that being mistaken for a Native American in the Upper Peninsula has, of course, made me feel more at home!

There is also a sub-culture that seems to cut across all socio-economic classes of Marquette. Judy's family has not been a part of this sub-culture because, according to Judy, her mom could never imagine herself keeping house in a retreat in the woods that *Yoopers* affectionately call "camp." But Judy, being an avid outdoors person and a lover of the woods, has always been receptive to the invitations of her friends whose families had the good fortune of owning such places in the woods. I describe it to explain the title for this section of the book, and also because it is a part of the cultural landscape that I am now aware of whenever I visit Marquette. As a matter of fact, I am told that the vacation cottage Judy and I now proudly own on the shore of Lake Superior in Marquette was once a "camp" for the previous owners. I have learned not to call our favorite plumber or barber on weekends for they would surely be unavailable. They would likely be out at their respective "camps" enjoying whatever *Yoopers* like to do in "da woods."

As I say a word or two about the title, "To da woods," seen on a bumper sticker I noticed on a few cars in Marquette, it is important to keep in mind that these are only the observations of an outsider. The Upper Peninsula of Michigan, known affectionately as the "UP" by its inhabitants (who call themselves *Yoopers*), is noted for its lakes, rivers, waterfalls, forests and wild life. I believe the wilderness, with its rugged beauty, has shaped the world view of *Yoopers*, who have made good use of their environment, especially the woods or "da woods." Growing up, they are sure to have pleasant memories of hiking, picking berries, hunting, fishing and camping. For high school students, "da woods" has special attractions for dating, especially for those so inclined to respond more readily to the call of nature. And for those who have reached maturity or "geezer-hood," as my brother-in-law Don calls it, "camp" provides an escape from the demands and pressures of living in the city, such as raking leaves, mowing the lawn, shaving regularly, or enduring the watchful scrutiny of a demanding spouse.

Whether the *Yoopers* today still represent the rugged pioneers of the old UP, or have become a more flabby and obese version from too much beer, fast food, *pasties*, and over-dependence on their SUVs and skidoos, "to da woods" still evokes memories that genuine *Yoopers* would not trade for anything. One good friend, a proud home-grown *Yooper*, made sure I did not forget that "an Upper Peninsula seven-course dinner is a *pasty* and a six-pack!" But aside from the food and drink, and the generous waistlines to show for it, their love for the outdoors tops it all. From the perspective of one of the Upper Peninsula's well-known citizens, jurist and author, Robert Traver, a retreat into the woods in pursuit of his favorite hobby, fly fishing for brook trout, was motivated by his "love (for) the environs where trout are found, which are invariably beautiful, and hate (for) the environs where crowds of people are found, which are invariably ugly; because of all the television commercials, cocktail parties, and assorted social posturing I thus escape . . ."

Equal devotion to the culture of the UP was expressed by a citizen writing to *The Mining Journal* (August 22, 2002), possibly as a warning to the many students of Northern Michigan University who were just arriving for another school year. He wrote:

> Concrete, asphalt, heavy traffic and visions of Traverse City are not perceived by everyone as 'improvement.' Don't assume we were waiting for you to arrive and 'save' us from our predicament. If you were born and raised here, then you have made the pilgrimage that is the birthright of many *Yoopers*. You moved away in order to discover the value of living north of the bridge.

With the appearance of shopping malls, the gradual disappearance of mom-and-pop corner stores, the beginnings of urban sprawl, trees being cut down by some homeowners (who want to make their front yard look like a Detroit suburb), and with more effort made to attract tourists who are discovering the secrets of "da woods," I wonder how long the rugged *Yoopers* can protect and maintain their wholesome way of life. I hope they will retain some of the traditions of the UP even as they extend their friendly and unadulterated welcome to visitors from south of the Mackinac Bridge. Never mind that when traveling at night on a lonely road in the UP, one might still get the impression that the only lighted place around is a bar, which is a serious concern for drivers, and certainly a liability for four-legged creatures on the road.

Although the UP offers such attractions as the rugged beauty of nature, the interesting history of abandoned mines, and the charm of old towns that seem to have been bypassed by time, not everyone is swayed by the beauty of the Upper Peninsula. Once, while driving through a small town in the remote Keweenaw Peninsula, Judy and I decided to stop at a house that advertised "antiques for sale." There were a few displays of odds and ends that were neatly arranged in what must have been the living room of an old house. A well-dressed woman, probably in her late 60s, approached and greeted us in what sounded like a thick European accent. As we looked around at the displays, I wondered about this woman because of her somewhat reserved bearing for the setting. She did not offer the usual chatty and informal "*Yooper*" welcome. As she was standing close by, I asked "Did I notice an elegant European accent?" She smiled, and replied briefly, "It eez. I am frrom Gerrmany." In an effort to find out more about her, I boldly inquired how she enjoyed living in the Keweenaw Peninsula. She held her head up, as if to distance herself from the setting, and said proudly with emphasis "I am frrom Berrlin, Gerrmany. Vat do you theenk!!"

"Barong by Pierre Cardin"

During one of my visits to the Philippines in the 1980s, I shopped in Manila to replace some of my older *Barong Tagalog*, handsome and dignified-looking traditional Philippine shirts. Although I wore a *Barong Tagalog* for special occasions, I also used one regularly when I taught at the university in late spring, during summer and in early fall. There were many choices, indeed, with a variety of colors and styles, including a cotton/synthetic fiber blend which is useful for traveling. It was a delight to see them all, except when the salesman offered to show me one that he thought was even better, but more expensive. "It was designed," he proudly announced, "by Pierre Cardin!" I reacted somewhat negatively, and probably not in a manner the salesman had expected. I commented we did not need Pierre Cardin to show us how to make a *Barong*. I added that those designed in the Philippines looked very good and elegant, and I was proud to wear them, but I was not interested in a European imitation. On that note, I thanked the salesman and continued my shopping elsewhere.

The incident reminded me once again how we, as consumers in the Philippines, have gravitated towards imported goods. As a former colony of the United States, the Philippine economy was developed as a supplier of raw materials and as a market for finished products. Historically, we exported raw materials, mainly to the United States. We bought back our raw materials as finished products. For example, cacao beans came back as chocolate bars, tobacco as cigarettes, and copra, that was used as an ingredient for many products, came back as soap and margarine. Based on the total yearly value of finished products the Philippines purchased from other countries, it was reported in *Kasaysayan* (1998) that importation by the Philippines of finished products from the United States rose from twelve percent of total imports in 1902 to sixty-six percent in 1936. Raw materials from the Philippines sold to the United States increased from forty percent in 1902 to seventy-nine percent in 1930. *(Kasaysayan, Vol. 6, p. 120)* Thus, in the absence of local industries that converted raw materials into finished products, it is understandable that Filipinos tended, initially, to depend upon imported goods. Aggressive and questionable advertising, such as giving out free samples of American cigarettes in busy streets and at college functions, also helped to promote sales of foreign products. Additionally, early attempts to produce products locally did not measure up to the quality of imported commodities, even for such items as pencils, safety pins, or cigarettes.

I remember an enterprising man from Laoag who wanted to take advantage of the forced scarcity of foreign products, a result of the Japanese occupation. He combined local materials to produce some commonly used items like ink, soap and soft drinks, products that were typically imported. Unfortunately, his *Buink*, a trade name which combined "Buisit," his family name, and "ink," did not quite succeed in the market. The water in the ink tended to separate from the dye, and two layers of colors were soon noticeable in the bottled products as they sat on the display shelves, gathering dust. His attempt to make soap was equally unsuccessful. For some reason, the bars of soap on display on the shelves sweated continuously and got smaller in the process. His venture into the soft drink business resulted in a concoction which he called *tinto dulce.* Unfortunately, it was the color of *mercurochrome,* an old liquid medicine used for small cuts and bruises. Because he had bottles and bottles of the *tinto dulce* that people did not want to buy, he "generously" donated them to somebody's political campaign for the many unsuspecting voters who went from one candidate's house to another, just to eat.

Father's attempt at entrepreneurship during the Japanese occupation was more successful than "*Bumanu*" (Buisit Manufacturing). Father was fond of American coffee. I remember different brands that he would bring home before the war: Chase & Sanborn, Maxwell House, Sanka, and Hills Brothers. So he had a lot of empty cans at the house that, I am sure, only increased his longing for his favorite drink. The roasted rice that we used for coffee during the war was certainly no substitute for regular coffee drinkers like Father, Uncle Damaso, other relatives and their friends.

When we were still living in the town of Solsona, Father was quite excited when some farmers, who usually trekked to the mountains east of town to gather firewood and barter with the mountain tribes, came back with stories about large avocadoes that were just spoiling on the ground. What particularly caught Father's interest was that the farmers also mentioned coffee berries littering the ground! "Coffee?" he inquired excitedly. "Do you know what coffee beans look like?" he pursued. He arranged to have the farmers take some used clothing to barter the next time they went to the mountains. He told them to bring back as much coffee as they could carry, and he would also give the farmers an extra commission. Sure enough, they brought back coffee. Father dried the coffee beans in the sun, removed the shells, and experimented with different ways of roasting and grinding until he got the desired result. He stored his newly roasted and ground coffee in his old coffee cans! Not quite Hills Brothers, but it was a lot better than roasted rice, to be sure!

On one of his trips to Laoag, Father visited relatives who used roasted rice in their "coffee shop." He brought samples of his own coffee and, as expected, he had as many orders as his supply could handle.

Although his experiment with roasting coffee was quite satisfying for him during that period, it did not diminish Father's yearning for imported coffee. Thus, for

Father, after the war one of the highlights of our return to normalcy was when "real coffee" became available again. I guess old and enjoyable habits are difficult to forget, but at that time, even younger people were subject to the attraction of imported goods. I mentioned earlier how Mother removed labels from Father's store-bought shirts and sewed them on the shirts she made for me so that, as I requested, they would be "just like some of the shirts my classmates had." The labels were "Manhattan," "Arrow," and "Van Heusen."

Maybe the attraction towards "imported" things is universal. I remember shopping in Sanaa, (North) Yemen, for a rug that was woven locally. I thought it would make a nice souvenir, just like the wall hangings I had bought in Lesotho in Southern Africa, which had native designs and were made out of local materials. To my disappointment, the vendors in Sanaa did not carry any locally woven rugs, but they took pride in offering me rugs "made in Belgium." At a seaside restaurant in Hodeida, Yemen, where they did not have any fresh fish listed on the menu, the waiter told me they had something better. They had "imported canned sardines from Portugal!" Asked why his films have become more popular in Europe, an American movie director jokingly replied "Maybe because people tend to like imported things."

It is a positive attitude for people to show interest in things and ideas that come from other cultures, and I do not see anything wrong in assimilating them for our own use, provided they are well adapted to local conditions. On the other hand, indiscriminate borrowing can also have unwanted consequences. I have wondered, for example, whether we have sufficiently adapted a western-style "democracy" in the Philippines. Given the country's problems, such as the high level of illiteracy, the limited educational opportunities for children in rural areas, the concentration of wealth in a small percentage of the population, and the entrenchment of the elite (who take turns running the country through violent elections with widespread allegations of voting irregularities), I seriously doubt that the substance of representative government has taken root as well as it should have. I say this regardless of how frequently the Philippines has been referred to as "America's showcase of democracy." Meanwhile the needs of the people, with the population exploding and the masses becoming increasingly poor, go unheeded. If this is the Philippines' version of "democracy" and it is not corrected soon, I think the "people power," popularized in the last couple of decades, will seem benign compared to what might be in store for us in the Philippines.

Meanwhile, I recognize that my reaction to "*barong* designed by Pierre Cardin" was probably a bit extreme. After all, the poor fellow was just trying to make a sale! But my response was conditioned by my view of the continued exploitation of developing countries by former colonizing countries turned industrial powers. On a personal level, I should also note that when I am in the Philippines where I can, from a distance, reflect on my experiences in the United States, I become more acutely aware of the challenges I have faced such as finding employment, pursuing a promotion, or second guessing the expectations of others when interacting with people socially. Given these perspectives, I feel more strongly that Filipinos should be proud of the things they can do well, including small things like making a *barong*. Such a reaction, I believe, has the effect of helping define the integrity of my cultural heritage, part of an anchor for who I am, and part of a mechanism to minimize the pressures of living between two cultures.

Obviously, this mechanism of adaptation and adjustment will vary from one person to another. Tanim Ansary's observation of how his siblings adapted differently to their American experience is a good illustration. He writes in his very interesting book, *West of Kabul, East of New York:* "Growing up bicultural is like straddling a crack. If the cultures are far apart, like those of Afghanistan and America, one feels an urge to get entirely to one side or the other. My siblings and I grew up with such divided souls, and we responded in different ways." (Ansary, p. 279) If this is an example of marginalization, I believe it is a tragedy of our society and our times that contact between cultures can breed divided loyalties, ambivalence and even cynicism instead of good will and cooperation. Memories of subjugation from history are not easily forgotten, and the continued exploitation of developing countries by industrial powers serves only to revive and exacerbate feelings of distrust between races and cultures.

Part IV

Professional Journey

The challenges of completing a degree pale in comparison to the obstacles of finding employment, especially for a racial minority, in the United States. Armed with a B.A. (1952) and an M.A. (1954) in Sociology from the University of the Philippines (UP), another M.A. in Sociology (1957) and a Ph.D. (1960) in Comparative Education from the University of Michigan (UM), plus five years of successful teaching (based on written student evaluations, both undergraduate and graduate students at UP and UM), I set out with confidence to apply for a teaching position at the college or university level. The procedure was to fill out a prescribed form for the "Placement Services" of UM, an office which duplicated and filed credentials for prospective employees. Those registered with the service were then notified of openings in their field and asked if they wished to be scheduled for an interview with visiting recruiters. I responded affirmatively to all who wished to see me for a college-level teaching position in social foundations of education. This was in 1960–1961.

Two colleges sought interviews with me. In the two sessions I had at Placement Services, I was told it would be desirable if I had elementary or secondary public school teaching experience in the United States, something I did not have. Although I thought the additional requirement was fair enough, it did not feel right that my fellow graduates in the same program at UM got placed, including one who did not have "public school teaching experience." This other graduate, who happened to be White, was hired by one of the colleges whose interviewer told me I needed public school experience!

The head of the department where I got my Ph.D. degree asked me later how I fared with the Placement Services. I told him I did not have much luck. He picked up the phone, called Placement Services to inquire how many openings in my field they had received. He was told that there were over twenty-five openings, that there were twelve applicants, and that all were hired, except one!

I decided I should have public school teaching experience and, given my credentials, I thought I should have no problem getting a job. The Ann Arbor Public School system was a logical place to apply since I was a resident of the city. In 1961, I had an appointment with the Director of Personnel for Ann Arbor Public Schools. He informed me that they preferred to hire only those with a teacher's certificate. It did not matter, he said, what other credentials I had. I knew very well that the Ann Arbor Public School system was hiring people without a certificate as substitute teachers, as long as they had a bachelor's degree. This practice has increased over the years in Michigan, as well as throughout the country, partly to cut costs.

Fortunately, the University of Michigan adjusted my full-time Lectureship to three-fourths time so that I could take courses to get a Michigan Teacher's Certificate. To do this, the clerk "assessed" my transcript and, in spite of five years of teaching at the university level, she decided I needed to take "Student Teaching," "Methods of Teaching Social Studies," and a "Seminar in Student Teaching."

I was a student teacher at Pioneer High School in Ann Arbor in 1961, earned my Michigan Teacher's Certificate, and was offered a full-time teaching position at the same senior high school. After completing one year of teaching, the high school offered me tenure to stay on as a teacher, which was quite unusual since, at that time, one was supposed to have at least two years of probationary teaching before tenure was granted. I felt honored, but declined since I was more interested in teaching at the university level.

My "big break" came after I presented a paper at a Mid-Western Conference of the Comparative Education Society, held in Ann Arbor at UM. The title of my paper was "Some Problems of Comparison and the Development of Theoretical Models in Comparative Education." It was well received at the conference and, immediately after my presentation, I was approached by representatives from three universities who inquired if I was looking for a teaching position. The three universities were McGill University in

Montreal, Canada, Syracuse University in New York, and the University of Hawaii.

I was invited to visit all three campuses, at their expense. After my visit to their respective campuses, each of these universities offered me a tenure-track position, but I turned them down for various reasons. Although McGill was my first choice, I still needed another year to meet the residency requirement for citizenship in the United States. Therefore, I could not leave the United States immediately for Canada. Meanwhile, McGill needed a faculty member right away in Comparative Education. When I was invited to Syracuse University to present a lecture, it was winter and the snowy setting did not appeal to me. As far as the University of Hawaii was concerned, I was worried about the possibility of being isolated professionally from the "mainland."

Ultimately I chose Eastern Michigan University (EMU), after I had been invited there by former UM classmates who were on the faculty at EMU. I took into account the fact that it had a good reputation in Teacher Education, and that EMU was located right next door to Ann Arbor. Ann Arbor was where we resided and it had a good public school system for our daughters, Cristina and Cynthia. Ann Arbor remains our hometown even now. Given all the opportunities I have had from EMU, in terms of overseas assignments, I know I made a good decision.

Before starting at EMU in the Fall of 1963, I applied to teach for the summer at North Carolina College, Durham, North Carolina, which was a predominantly African American institution, both in terms of its faculty and its student population. Discussions with my students and with professional African American educators, who expressed their views candidly about American society and education, were informative and eye-opening experiences. It was a very pleasant and useful professional interlude for me before I assumed a tenure track position at Eastern Michigan University.

My experience with racism in higher education did not end with my new position at EMU. After a few years at EMU, I decided I wanted to apply for a leave of absence, so that I could find some time to work abroad, to strengthen my background in comparative education. One way of doing this was to teach in the United States Department of Defense Dependents Schools (DODDS), which were located overseas. The possibility of pursuing this plan for professional development appeared to me to be viable when one of my summer students, an African American, informed me that he was a Social Studies teacher stationed in Germany. He added that they were in need of more Social Studies teachers, and he encouraged me to apply, if I was interested in a year or two of professional experience abroad. Since I already had my teacher's certificate and public school experience, I submitted my application to the Placement Center at UM. I was notified by UM when the DODDS recruiter would be on campus, and was asked if I would like to schedule an interview. I informed the UM that I would and the date and time were set.

When I showed up for my appointment, the interviewer looked a bit surprised. At first she said, "There must be a mistake." I assured her that I had an appointment, and showed her the notice from UM. Obviously uneasy about the situation, she asked me to sit down as she looked through her file. Sure enough, she had my file. She looked at my credentials for a while. Then she started shaking her head, indicating, I suppose, that she found something undesirable. She said "You have a Michigan Teacher's Certificate in Social Studies, but you do not have the right distribution of courses!" It seemed to me that she had found an excuse to reject my application, after going through a token interview.

To be technical about it, I believe that under our federal system of government, education in the public schools, as well as teacher certification, are under the jurisdiction of the states with their "reserved powers", and not under the federal government with its "delegated powers," as provided in the Tenth Amendment of the United States Constitution. This has been the established and accepted application of the Tenth Amendment in relation to teacher certification. Accordingly, it was not within the authority of a federal clerk to evaluate "distribution of courses" of a teacher's certificate that had been duly approved according to state requirements. I left the charade of the interview feeling angry and disgusted.

The following summer, my graduate student, who was teaching in Germany, came to see me. He told me that he had gone through the appointees for Social Studies and did not find my file. Had I changed my mind? I told him what had happened at the interview. With expletives from a truly angry person, he exclaimed, "That is exactly what I went through! When will they stop!" That time, through a representative of the federal government, discrimination and racism had reared their ugly heads once again.

I believe racial minorities in the United States will continue, in their professional life, to be occasionally subjected to discrimination, in various forms. Short of quitting, my advice is to do your work to the best of your ability. In the work setting, stand up for what you believe in, but select the issues that are worth fighting for and, finally, maintain a strong stomach in order to stay the course.

"I Was a Kindergarten Dropout" is a short review of how my attitude towards education changed over time. I am thankful to the people who had the patience and confidence in me, despite a few shakes of the head from some of my teachers in grade and high schools, who expressed frustration and dire predictions for my future.

"Don't Argue With Me, Samonte" deals with varieties of parochialism and dogmatism in my education. The story includes some impressions from my early education in the Philippines and some isolated incidents at UP and at UM.

"I Have Been to Honolulu" is a recollection of some of the social stereotypes I encountered in connection with my professional activities. These were little irritations, to be sure, so I dealt with them with humor and/or rationalization and then got on with life's more serious encounters.

"The Expert" is a short account of some of my professional experiences overseas. These assignments provided me with opportunities to participate in programs in Cyprus, England, Honduras, Swaziland, and (North)

Yemen. These were the highlights of my professional journey. The assignments in Swaziland and North Yemen were United States Foreign Aid projects.

"Exploring Distant Shores" is about my contact with fellow Filipinos, whom I met while working overseas. They were not just social contacts, for some sought my advice in dealing with what they perceived as problems of abuse, and having contracts that were not fully honored by their employers. In spite of their difficulties, most of the Filipinos I met and worked with overseas represented their country well with the high quality of their work. I was proud to be one of them.

I Was a Kindergarten Dropout

Peering apprehensively through the door that was slightly ajar, I scrutinized the fearsome-looking guests of *Lolo* Nicolas Segundo. To a three-year-old, the deep-set eyes separated by a sharp nose on a hairy face of each of the four men definitely looked malevolent. I was puzzled, however, that *Lolo* Nicolas did not seem to be afraid of them. As a matter of fact, they all seemed to be having a wonderful time laughing and conversing in Spanish. I learned later that *Lolo* was a lawyer for the *Tabacalera*, a Spanish corporation that dealt with the tobacco business in the Philippines. The guests were *Lolo* Nicolas' clients.

My reactions to his guests must have been influenced partly by the ghost stories my elders narrated to me many times. Intended as entertainment for kids, these folk tales usually featured a spirit that could inflict mischief and/or harm on misbehaving children! One such spirit was the *sinan*

Castila (like a Spaniard) who, so the story went, could change in size, move from one place to another with the speed of light, or could vanish into thin air. Other tales described a white hairy leg hanging from a tree.

I learned later that ghost stories were not only for the children's entertainment. There were older folks who actually believed in them as well. I recall going with *Lola* Sabina, Father's mother, to her favorite drinking place, two houses down from the old Samonte house. In the evening, sitting on two bamboo benches which faced each other under a *nipa* awning, three or four of her drinking buddies would chat while they enjoyed their *basi* (sugar cane wine). *Baket* Anneng sold this basi by the glass at two *centavos* a shot. As the consumption of the *basi* increased, so did their claims about personal "sightings" of the *sinan Castila*. When the group finally broke up, a bit inebriated at that point, each would go on his/her separate and merry way along the dimly lit street, possibly to experience more "sightings." Then they would all be back at *Baket* Anneng's the following day to tell about it!

Meanwhile, back to the Segundo house where I was looking at four *Castilas* in our living room! All I could do was look, breathe quietly, and wait for them to leave. Unfortunately, they came to the house regularly, so I kept my distance from them. One day, while playing alone at the entry to the house, I was caught unaware of their approach until they were just two meters away from me. I turned around and there I was, face-to-face with the four *Castilas*!

They said something which sounded like "*Hola*," but I screamed and ran into one of the rooms as fast as I could. I heard them laugh as I closed the door behind me.

At age six it was time to enroll in kindergarten. It was decided that I would attend the Holy Ghost Academy (now called "Holy Spirit") where Auntie Anching and Auntie Angeles, Mother's younger sisters, were also pupils in elementary school. I was accompanied by *Lola* Leoncia on my first day of school, and I met Miss Cid, who was the lay teacher. I was surprised to also be introduced to the "Mother Superior" who, I was positive, was a *Castila*! I moved behind *Lola* quickly, but peeked around and studied the Mother Superior more closely. Like the *Castilas*, she had the same deep-set eyes, separated by a sharp nose, but she did not have a beard. She was dressed in a black gown, had a stiff cowl that draped over her shoulders, and had a large crucifix that dangled from her neck. It was then that I began to doubt whether I would like school after all, in spite of the pep talk at home telling me how much fun it would be. Fortunately, the lay teacher took charge of most of the classes while a nun came to the classroom every day only to teach religious education. With forty other children in the classroom, I figured I was safe enough from the nuns, and I was soon enjoying doing a lot of projects, learning about Aesop's fables and, of course, going out at recess.

The convent where the school was located was a two-story cement and brick building. Its walls were at least a meter thick. It had high ceilings and long dark corridors. It looked very much like the other buildings around the town plaza

First day in Kindergarten

that had been constructed during the Spanish period. The convent was connected to the Roman Catholic Church, which was an impressive structure that dominated the courtyard. Coseteng notes in her book (p. 15) that:

> The church as the House of God was not only for worship or for listening to the exhortations of the curate from the pulpit, but also was the visible proof of the stability and permanence, if not power, of the new religion. Aside from serving as sanctuary for those who have broken the law or were evading arrest, its solid walls also provided safety in times of danger and natural disasters.

It was under the shade of these buildings and a number of *acacia* trees in the courtyard where we played during recess, and where we assembled before going back into our classrooms. Mornings started with a prayer in the classroom, recess ended with a prayer in church, and each school day closed with another prayer.

However, my religious education did not end there. Auntie Anching and Auntie Angeles, who were four and two years older than I, respectively, made sure that I knew about guardian angels, devils, heaven, purgatory, hell, and mortal sins. They showed me illustrations of heaven with angels sitting on the clouds playing the harp. By way of contrast, they had a picture of hell that, I was told, was a destination for misbehaving kids. It puzzled me, however, that the devils were usually portrayed as if they were having a wild party and having a good time. Consequently, the two contrasting illustrations presented a confusing choice for me. And this was compounded by the fact that I was afraid of heights and, therefore, could not imagine myself sitting up there in heaven, on a cloud, playing the harp.

While I was not sure how seriously I should take all that business about heaven, purgatory and hell, I welcomed the new attention from my aunts and being allowed to play with them in their doll house, which was a little *nipa* hut in the garden. Auntie Anching and Auntie Angeles had dolls made out of rolled pieces of cloth, tied in two parts where another roll was inserted for the arms. The dolls were of different sizes to represent parents, friends and children. They had pretend dialogues of visiting dolls, serving *merienda*, reminding the children to observe their manners, etc. Other girls from the neighborhood would come and play with the dolls, too. I thought one of them was rather pretty, and I enjoyed sitting next to her. I was very disappointed when my aunts decided not to let me play with them when spots started appearing on my face. Can you imagine, I reflected angrily, keeping me from playing with them just because of some little spots on my face? This started a malevolent plot, to which I am now ashamed to admit.

Because I was homebound until my spots went away, I had an opportunity to visit the doll house while my aunts were in school. This time I brought my mother's sewing scissors with me. I entered the dollhouse, picked up the cloth dolls and cut off their heads! Having accomplished this murderous act, I went back to my sick bed. How my aunts screamed when they got home from school and discovered the massacre at their dollhouse! With all the wailing, I decided I'd better move to another location. I crawled underneath my bed. While I am sure my aunts concluded then and there that I was probably the culprit, I do not remember any scolding from Mother or *Lola* Leoncia. As a matter of fact, it was not discussed in the family, at least not in my presence. I did notice that when I chanced upon my uncles or Father looking at me, they looked the other way, trying to keep a straight face.

Returning to school was a refreshing change from being confined to bed. I learned that some of my classmates had the spots, too.

The weeks passed uneventfully. I do not remember what I was doing when, one day, the nun told me to pay attention. She stopped the religious education temporarily and started to walk towards me! My fear of the *Castila* came rushing back to me! I stood up quickly and went to the opposite side of the table, away from the nun. I circled the table to keep my distance from her as she followed me. The other pupils began watching. The nun hailed two other nuns, who happened to pass by along the corridor. As they quickened their steps towards me with their head covers billowing in the air like the wings of bats, I eyed the door, dashed quickly toward it and ran down the corridor. With three nuns in pursuit, I ran until I got out of the building. I walked home from there, a kindergarten dropout. Mother asked why I was home early. I do not remember what I told her, but she and Father probably got a report later from the school. The family decided that I should wait until the next school year, when I turned seven, to enroll in the public school where *Mamu* Ti, the disciplinarian, was the school principal.

Over the years I have revisited these episodes of years past. I have reflected, for example, on how my attitudes towards racial differences were shaped at an early age, and how they changed over time. Myths and half-truths, told and re-told, have no doubt influenced me. Ghost stories and the central casting of the *Castila* in the spirit world were influential. Stories about spirits were very much a part of my childhood as a form of entertainment, especially when told skillfully. More than that, sometimes they were used as a means of enforcing discipline. I remember, for example, how

I had been encouraged to eat my vegetables, to stay away from the trees at noon, to go to bed early, to brush my teeth, etc., or else! It was no help that there were superstitious adults who actually believed in *sinan Castila* and that sort of thing. Thus, my stereotype about the Spaniards carried over to the Caucasian nuns at the Holy Ghost Academy where I attended kindergarten.

Progressing through the higher grades in elementary school helped make me aware of other perspectives. My introduction to the study of science broadened my world view. It was very different from the simplified conceptualization of religion that I was taught in kindergarten. Learning how to read gave me more flexibility in exploring ideas on my own. As I spent more time with the extended family on my father's side, there was more talk, in very positive terms, about "America" and about *Americanos*. Uncle Damaso, Father's older brother, had just returned from the United States, where he had earned a medical degree from Loyola University in Chicago. He entertained us with stories about his experiences "in America." I saw American visitors who occasionally came to the Samonte house or at the Mission Hospital when I accompanied Uncle Damaso when he visited some of his patients. It helped, too, that I could understand what they were saying, quite unlike when *Lolo* Nicolas chatted with his visitors in Spanish. More conversations about America at the Samonte table, and about Uncles Fort, Larry, and Johnny, who were then in Chicago, were endlessly fascinating to me.

Working with American GIs when I was an orderly at a United States airbase in Gabu, just outside my hometown, impressed me, too, in a positive way. I saw the American GIs as hard workers, a characteristic I was taught in my family as a sign of good character. Although movies from Hollywood were influential, they presented a glamorized and distorted image of American society. It is probably worth noting, too, that Father and Mother's generation went to school during the American occupation of the Philippines. I was, therefore, a scion of an age group that tended to be pro-American. One of the results of these influences was that, by the time I completed grade school, I had a more tolerant attitude toward people who did not look like me.

Going to America to study "just like Uncle Damaso" became a consuming ambition of mine. I explored various ways to finance my way to the United States. While still in the high school, a recruiter looking for laborers for the sugarcane plantations in Hawaii came to Laoag. I figured I could work and finish my high school education in Hawaii. That would enable me, I reasoned, to save money and provide for my college education later on. Father discouraged me from pursuing this line of action. He cautioned that I ran the risk of not ever finishing my high school education. So, I completed my high school in Laoag, and enrolled at the University of the Philippines. After finishing a bachelor's program, I decided to pursue a graduate degree. It was while I was a graduate student that I was informed about a bilateral agreement between the Philippines and the United States that allowed the U.S. to recruit a specified number of young Filipinos for the U.S. Navy and the U.S. Army. Figuring I could serve the minimum required years of service, I would then earn scholarship money for education at a college or university in the U.S. I sent an application to the United States Naval Base in Cavite, and received a reply instructing me to go to Cavite to complete the application process, including a physical examination.

It was about that time, however, that I was offered two scholarships for graduate education in the United States. One was from a grant in connection with the Institute of Public Administration, which was being developed under a foreign aid program from the United States government at the University of the Philippines (UP). The other was from the University of the Philippines, which had a program to select some of its own new graduates for scholarships abroad for advanced studies to become future faculty members of the UP. I dropped all ideas about joining the U.S. Navy at that point, but choosing between a U.S. scholarship and a Philippine scholarship was not easy. I opted for the scholarship offered by the University of the Philippines.

The UP scholarship ultimately brought me to the University of Michigan, where I completed a graduate program, and where I met, courted and married Judith Elzinga from Marquette, Michigan. She was then an undergraduate student at the University of Michigan, majoring in cultural anthropology. I should note that Judy is of Dutch, Belgian, French and German descent and could certainly pass for a blue-eyed *Castila*! Aside from a more positive change in my attitude towards other races, it helped, too, that she looked far more attractive than those bearded visitors of *Lolo* Nicolas! I stayed in Michigan to pursue an academic career, and raise a family. We have two lovely daughters, Cristina and Cynthia, and a grandson, Brooklyn, who is growing up to be a fine young man.

"Don't Argue with Me, Samonte"

Valiantly trying to fend off the seductive call of siesta time, I sat through an undergraduate history class at the University of the Philippines while the professor droned on with a monotonous and dry lecture on United States foreign policy in the Philippines. Hearing him declare that "The Philippines is the showcase of democracy in the Orient," I became energized enough to raise my hand. Lifting his eyebrows and peering at me above his glasses, he looked irritated by the interruption, "Yes, Samonte?" Although somewhat intimidated, I managed to ask whether he thought we really had democracy in the Philippines. After a short pause, which seemed like an eternity, the other members of the class shifted their attention towards me. He responded, "Unlike some other developing countries, we have free elections in the Philippines, don't we!" Not satisfied with the answer, and not wanting to be dismissed so easily by him, I countered "But, Sir, we are told that only a small percentage of the population vote, and it was reported in the newspapers that there were widespread cases of bribery and intimidation of voters in the last national election." He removed his glasses, as if to emphasize the impertinence of my comment, and he thundered "Don't argue with me, Samonte!"

Fortunately, this was an isolated incident. The faculty members I had at the University of the Philippines, most of whom had graduate degrees from top universities in the United States and Europe, were very much in command of their respective subjects and were open-minded. As a matter of fact, at that time the University of the Philippines was regarded as having a rigorous program, and being a top-quality institution of higher education in the Philippines, as well as in Southeast Asia. But the incident that one afternoon did remind me of the authoritarianism, discipline, drill and memorization that tended to dominate my elementary and secondary education in the Philippine public schools.

After completing a master's degree from the University of the Philippines, I got ready for my trip to the United States as a recipient of a government scholarship. In this connection, some Americans who were at the University of the Philippines, either as Fulbright scholars or members of a United States foreign aid program, made it a point to remind those of us preparing to go abroad, to ask questions and participate in class discussions. That advice was obviously prompted by their observations that some of our faculty members were more authoritarian than those in the

United States, and that students tended to be relatively passive. I appreciated their advice, and I was determined to be an active class participant at Michigan.

However, it was more difficult than I thought to participate in graduate class discussions during my first semester at the University of Michigan (UM). In order to follow the meaning of the discussion, I tended to go through a specific process. I would translate what I heard in English into *Ilocano* (one of many dialects in the Philippines). In formulating a reaction, be it a question or comment, I would go through the same process of translating from *Ilocano* to English. By the time I was done with the switch from one language to the other, the discussion had already moved on to other topics. Thus, my intention to be an active class participant was deferred for a few semesters, not only because of the language problem but also because of the need to change my mental process from memorization to critical analysis. The graduate classes in the Social Sciences required more analysis than just parroting definitions. Unfortunately, my education in the Philippines did not adequately prepare me for that. There were, to be sure, some teachers during my early education who emphasized a more practical and analytical approach, but they were the exceptions.

I finally made the difficult adjustment to a more fluent use of English, and also to a more analytical approach to my studies. This was followed by my appointment as a Teaching Fellow, while I was still a graduate student. I had responsibilities for teaching an undergraduate course in Educational Sociology for juniors and seniors at UM. After completing my

Ph.D. in comparative education, I was appointed full-time Lecturer in the School of Education at UM. As Lecturer, I had the responsibility of teaching two undergraduate courses in education, in addition to one master's level course in History of Education, Sociology of Education, or Comparative Education; and a doctoral level course for students working on their Ph.D. in Comparative Education.

As Lecturer, I sometimes assisted one of the senior faculty members in a doctoral seminar. It was in this assignment that I encountered once again a form of parochialism. I thought I had all of that behind me, after that undergraduate history class at the University of the Philippines about ten years earlier, but there it was in the doctoral seminar in which I was assisting at the University of Michigan! The senior faculty in the doctoral seminar had a private conference with me. He told me he did not want me to disagree with him in front of the students! Surprised that I should find such an attitude at a university with a world-class reputation for high standards, I asked if I was mistaken in my understanding that the seminar was a place to encourage and discuss different ideas. I suggested later that I could not in good conscience continue to participate in such a seminar. In taking such a stand, I knew full well that any hope I had of being recommended to a tenure track position in the UM Education faculty was in jeopardy. I gave that some thought, but decided on standing by what I thought was right, despite the fact that two faculty members, friends of mine, came to warn me of such a possibility.

I hasten to add that my general experience at the University of Michigan, as a student, was a very positive one. I have not allowed that isolated incident in the seminar, where I was asked to put up a façade of agreement with a senior faculty member, to cloud my belief in the role of universities as a meeting place for different ideas.

Unfortunately, some form of dogmatism will always be a part of our social, political and intellectual environment, and we deal with it when it intrudes into our life. Students of history would not easily forget, for example, the conflict generated by the Inquisition in European history, the McCarthy era in the U.S., and the pursuit of a foreign policy that was as brutal as in Vietnam, supposedly in defense of "democracy."

Needless to say, narrow-mindedness does not have to come in global proportions, as these examples might imply. We know it can also be found in small places from even smaller people. On rare occasions, there were misguided faculty members who thought their instructional materials and methods should be adopted by others based on the questionable reasoning that what worked for them would also work for others. While I think sharing of ideas between faculty members is a good thing and should be encouraged, imposing one's ideas over others is an entirely different matter. I believe conformity is anathema to the principle of free inquiry especially in a university. For the very rare occasions that I encountered situations like this, I resisted them.

Fortunately, most of the colleagues I have worked with exemplified intellectual maturity and integrity; they respected diversity and individuality. They were faculty members who gave substance to what the academy was supposed to be as a market place for ideas. But whenever dogmatism reared it ugly head, I would remind myself once again of that wonderful saying which goes something like this: "I seek the fellowship of those who are in search of the truth, but I avoid the company of those who claim to have found it!" With gratitude to the scholar who coined this statement, it has been an effective source of balance for me whenever I am haunted by that voice from the distant past: "Don't argue with me, Samonte!"

Coffee break for teachers at Ann Arbor Pioneer High School where I taught to "gain public school experience." 1962.

With the US Ambassador to Swaziland explaining the Mobile Teacher Center and its introduction to Swaziland. 1980.

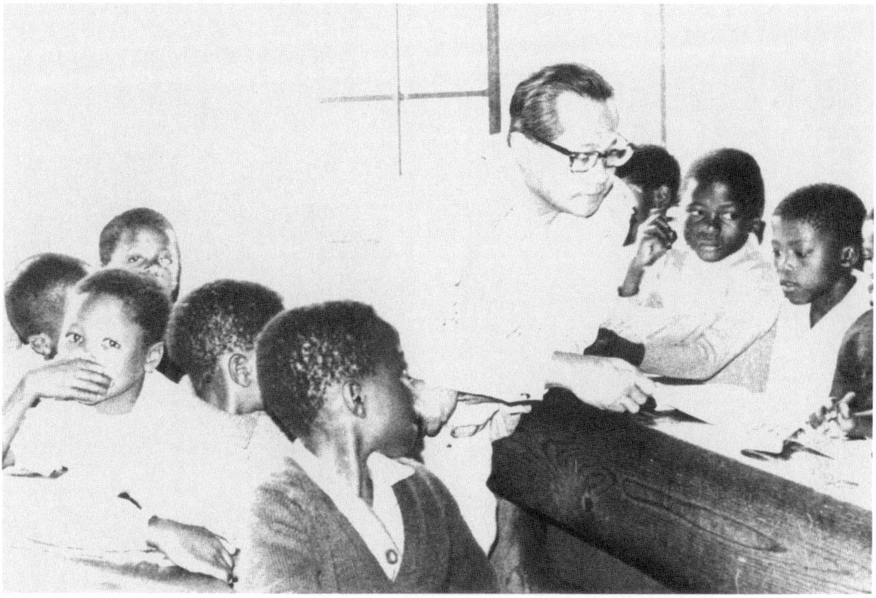

Visiting school children in Swaziland. 1979.

Visiting school children in Swaziland. 1979.

Field trip in a village near Hodeida, North Yemen. 1984.

Field trip to the highlands of North Yemen. 1985.

"Oh, Yes, I Have Been to Honolulu"

It did not seem too long ago that I had been on horseback returning from one of the remote villages of the province of Iloilo. I had just completed my portion of a literacy survey for the University of the Philippines. Soon it would be time to return to Manila and get ready for my first trip to the United States as a student, the fulfillment of a life-long ambition! Two months later, I was sitting at a Thursday afternoon tea for foreign students at the International Center of the University of Michigan (UM). It was only two or three weeks into the 1954 Fall semester at the UM, where I had enrolled for graduate studies under a scholarship from the Philippine government. Since I did not know many people then, I looked forward to the weekly tea for a bit of social activity. It was a good excuse to dress up a bit and wear the new sport coat and woolen slacks that my Uncle Larry in Chicago had bought for me. I was also hoping that there would be young ladies at the tea which, to be truthful, was probably my main reason for attending. Unfortunately, most of the foreign students at the event were men who, I suspect, were there for the same reason. Instead of sweet young things, the women at the tea were matronly. They were, we were told, wives of faculty members of the university.

The women made the rounds with their plates of cookies, exchanged pleasantries with the students and moved on. When one of them got to me, she asked where I was from as I picked a cookie from her plate. “I am from the Philippines, Ma’am,” I answered. Perhaps recognizing an opening for a little conversation, she said “Oh, yes, I have been to Honolulu!” I hastened to make the correction that the Philippines was on the other side of the Pacific Ocean. “Oh, what difference does it make.” she responded with a little shrug of her shoulders and moved on to the next student to spread good will and international understanding. Needless to say, I was a bit dumbfounded. I rationalized and dismissed it as a harmless irritation, much like having pebbles in one’s shoe.

A few more minor experiences included being asked “How are you?” At first, I thought it was an unmistakable invitation to talk. Wrong! If I happened to respond in the nature of reciting some of my aches and pains, or being behind in writing my papers as a student, or receiving a parking ticket, etc, and I got a reply of “How nice!” I soon got the message that either they were not listening or they didn’t care one bit! I suppose if we can deal with these little irritations with a sense of humor and rationalization, we can probably dismiss them and forget about them.

Being occasionally greeted as "Ranjit," "Kish" or "Kim," by colleagues who I thought knew me well enough as "Ric" was disappointing or amusing. "Ric," my nickname since coming to the United States, was a concession to my American friends who seemed to have difficulty remembering my first name, "Quirico". It usually came out as "Queer-ko," "Kirko," or "Quirk-ko." On the other hand, I, too, have caught myself mixing up names of some colleagues. I do not remember how many times I have greeted "Sue" when I should have said "Betty," or "Jack" when I should have said "Lou." What made it awkward was when I realized my mistake from the surprised look of the person, and he or she was too polite to tell me that I had done it again. I guess the "they-all-look-alike" perspective works both ways and if we recognized this, we would be more forgiving.

I became a naturalized United States citizen in 1962 at a ceremony that took place at the County building in Ann Arbor. It was attended by family members of inductees and by other visitors. After the oath was administered, the families moved forward to congratulate the new citizens. Among the visitors were some elderly ladies who carried tiny American flags. One of them approached me and, with a smile, she congratulated me and handed me a flag. She identified herself as a "Daughter of the American Revolution." My initial reaction to the lady was bewilderment, for I remember that I made a quick calculation how old she must have been. Just the same, I bowed slightly and thanked her graciously. When I got home, a little more thought dispelled any foolish notion I had that anybody could live for so long! Of course, I should have known better. Filipinos, too, are noted for their propensity for organizations named "Sons and Daughters of Ilocos Norte," and "Sons of Ilocos Sur." As if that is not enough, we also have "Sons of Batac," "Sons of Laoag," etc. Just take a look at the roster of Filipino organizations in any large American city. You will realize what a fragmented country the Philippines is. I should add that these designations of Filipino organizations should never be equated with the American expression "S.O.B."

There are other situations, however, that cannot be easily dismissed by humor, rationalization or a little bit of research. A friend from the Philippines, who was a scientist and stood barely five feet tall, had a different problem adjusting to American culture. He confessed he felt very insignificant when talking to people, especially when he came up only to their armpit! Although he was recognized as very capable in his profession, the problem bothered him to such an extent that he decided to return to the Philippines for good. In a way, the Philippines has this man's unusual "armpit complex" to thank, since, upon his return, the country gained a highly productive man of science.

Although materials on cultural diversity can, no doubt, be a gold mine for education, I believe American teachers need to be more knowledgeable about other cultures, and be more analytical, instead of just focusing on holidays, recipes and stereotypes. Additionally, adjustment to a new culture is probably easier if it can be a two-way process. Humor and rationalization can serve as buffers up to a point, and mutual understanding can help dispel stereotyping. But some degree of accommodation of each other's cultural differences, if that is possible, would be a more significant and meaningful process of adjustment. Unfortunately our political system and our academic institutions appear more inclined to accommodate groups that have political and economic clout, which helps sustain those who are in power. At any rate, I hope the faculty wife who had visited Honolulu bothered to check that Honolulu is not in the Philippines.

The "Expert"

The young attractive woman approached me and introduced herself as a member of the Swedish International Development Agency. It was a mild summer afternoon under the jacaranda trees, which were in lavender bloom, and a cocktail party was in progress for members of the various foreign aid missions to the Kingdom of Swaziland. This was in 1979, and I was a member of an education project funded by the United States Agency for International Development, administered by Eastern Michigan University for the Swaziland Ministry of Education. After exchanging pleasantries, she asked: "In what field are you an expert?" I had never considered myself an "expert" for the term implied a lot of responsibility, and I also found it presumptuous to be so labeled in a developing country. I was, therefore, unprepared for the question. Taking mental note that she was attractive and refined, I did not wish to be contentious. I gave a general and vague response indicating that I was an "adviser," my official title in relation to the Swaziland Ministry of Education. She did not follow-up, so I asked her the same question. Without hesitation, she responded, "I am an expert in Biology." For one who looked young enough to be a recent college graduate, I admired her confidence. Such an attitude on the part of foreign aid agents, however, has been an issue I have struggled with as an academician, even more so at that time since I was a member of a foreign aid team.

This question relates to a bigger issue about the role of donor countries. Is it the intent, for instance, to impose the culture of the donor on the client country, and if so, to what extent and in what way? It is reasonable to say that the extension of foreign aid is generally motivated by the donor country's national interest, and the United States is no exception. It would be naive to assume otherwise.

I remain dubious about government claims regarding promotion of "self-determination" or "democracy" in developing countries. I questioned, for example, what democracy we were protecting in Kuwait when the United States unleashed "Desert Storm." I wondered if it was just to insure the availability of the oil supply for American industries and to help maintain our extravagant life style. Clearly the donor country could be interested in a number of things, such as access to natural resources, markets, and bases for air or naval operations. It is not surprising, therefore, that differences with a friendly client country are often relegated to the background. Issues such as violations of national sovereignty, persecution of selected religious groups and human rights abuses are ignored as long as the donor can get what it wants from the client country.

It appears that the United States has been willing to work with dictators as long as those dictators served the agenda of the United States. And if we believe some sources, the U.S. has conveniently helped get rid of these same dictators when they were no longer cooperative or needed. Remember the United States support for Batista of Cuba, the Shah of Iran, Marcos of the Philippines, Noriega of Panama, Pinoche of Chile, and Saddam Hussein of Iraq. As long as they served American interests, they remained in power, only to have the United States help get rid of them later.

If we need to be more concerned about the image Americans project abroad, the signs of improvement do not appear to be forthcoming. Recently, in a letter to the editor of *TIME* (January 21, 2002) a writer criticized what he called our "insensitivity to others." Quoted in full:

> In your article 'Inside *Tora Bora*' you stated that 'the Afghans might be useful proxies for some jobs but were perhaps not quite professional enough to finish the war against the *Taliban*' (The Manhunt, Dec. 24). That remark was offensive and belittling toward those Afghan soldiers who in the past weeks shed their blood in battle in their homeland. Most of America's ground forces have seen relatively little action during that time, while the 'not quite professional' Afghan troops have cleared out the *Taliban* and *al-Qaeda*. Such insensitivity to others and a tendency to self-aggrandizement often lead to hatred of the U.S. in other parts of the world.

An article by Robin Wright and Mark Magnier of the *Los Angeles Times* (*Ann Arbor News*, February 19, 2002) reviewed samples of reactions to the much-ridiculed "axis of evil" phrase spoken by President Bush in his State of the Union Address in 2002. "The Japanese daily *Asahi Shimbun* has charged that Bush's comments have increased regional tensions and displayed a complete disregard for local sensitivities, while *Okinawa Times* said the United States is following a misguided law-of-the-jungle approach". Wright and Magnier continued with a quotation from Kazuto Suzuki, a professor at Tsukuba University: "It underscores the rather childish U.S. diplomacy. He has thrown up a stereotype, but there is no hard evidence behind his charges."

From a more personal perspective, I remember visits to the Philippines in the 1980s and 90s when I encountered young Filipino college students who were more nationalistic than my generation. They were only too glad to tell me (particularly me, who had renounced my Philippine citizenship to become an American citizen) that the Philippines had been on the short end of the stick in its relationship with the United States. They cited the pollution left by United States Armed Forces in the naval bases in Cavite and Subic Bay, and at the airbase Clark Field. They also called my attention to the indiscriminate use by American corporations of pesticides (even those banned from use in the United States), and to the distribution of free samples of American cigarettes, at college functions and in the streets of Manila. They asked me why pharmaceutical drugs that could not be sold without prescription in the United States could be purchased over the counter in Filipino drug stores! These young people's anger was unmistakable.

There is also a growing interest among Filipino historians to learn more about alleged atrocities committed by American soldiers in the Philippines at the turn of the 20th century. One such effort is a documentary entitled "Memories of a Forgotten War: A Documentary on the Philippine American War of 1899." This is the work of two filmmakers, Camilla Benoliar Griggers, a Filipino American born and raised in California, and Sari Raissa Lluch, who was raised and educated in the Philippines. The documentary premiered at the University of the Philippines in January, 2002. Some examples of artistic ventures on the Philippine American war include F. Sionil Jose's novel, *Dusk*, which includes a brief description of the alleged massacre of villagers by American soldiers in the town of Baugen, Ilocos Sur, and John Chode's play, *A Howling Wilderness*, which is based on the military trial of officers involved in mass killings against Filipinos in other regions of the Philippines. This play opened in New York one week before the September 11, 2001, attacks, but closed shortly after.

My observations in other developing countries that Judy and I visited in the 1980s reminded me of the anger I encountered in the Philippines. For example, after the United States Armed Forces "intervened" in Granada, presumably to "save" the people of Granada from themselves, I took a trip with Judy to that country in 1985. We saw conspicuously marked buildings with "Go Home Yankee" graffiti. It was not too different, I should add, from some of the graffiti, like "*Fuera* Yankee," that I noticed on buildings in Honduras in the late 1980s, when I was sent there on a short work assignment.

In retrospect, I think people in developing countries tend to react negatively, not so much against the American people in general, but more against pronouncements from our government leaders, which may be perceived as insensitive. Policies are sometimes viewed as being designed primarily in terms of the United States' national interests, such as the exploitation of resources, markets and labor in developing countries. But it is also understandable when some people in other countries react negatively against what they regard as loud and rowdy behavior of some of our servicemen and some of our tourists abroad. Once, while my guide and I were riding on a bus in Seoul, South Korea, some American soldiers boarded the bus. They were talking loudly and seemed oblivious that there were other people on the bus; the other passengers looked at them with disdain. My tourist guide leaned over and whispered, "These people behave as if they own the world!"

I was reminded of that unpleasant situation in Korea a year later in Mannheim, Germany. This time it involved American professionals! I was invited to give a presentation at a conference of American educators in Mannheim, Germany. In the evening, about ten of the conferees decided to go out to dinner and they invited me to go along with them. We went to a small but elegant restaurant. The place was conservatively and tastefully decorated. The local customers were well dressed; the women were nicely attired for an evening out and the men wore coats and ties. The couples chatted quietly by candle light. Our group entered the place noisily and apparently unmindful of the other people in that setting. The Americans had some of the tables rearranged so they could all sit together. I saw the same disapproving and angry look from the other customers in that restaurant as I saw among the passengers in that bus in Korea! I wished then that I had gone out on my own to enjoy a nice quiet dinner somewhere! Although these are admittedly minor incidents, they reflect how Americans who behave insensitively are sometimes regarded abroad.

How some people, here and abroad, regard what they view as a pro-Israel United States policy in relation to the Israeli-Palestinian conflict has not been very helpful either in our effort to win friends and influence people. As one member of the Ann Arbor Jewish community wrote recently to the *Ann Arbor News* (November 16, 2003):

> Readers should be reminded that Israel is currently in violation of over 60 such UN Resolutions, and it is our U.S. taxes and funding that allow Israel to maintain its illegal occupation of the West Bank, Gaza and East Jerusalem. September 11, 2001 happened, and we wonder why there is so much hatred against the United States!

With the tragedy of that fateful day, September 11th, as a catalyst and/or an excuse, the United States is now engaged in an ill-advised preemptive war, initiated by the President of the United States, supposedly to "bring democracy and freedom to the people of Iraq." However one rationalizes the war in Iraq, it is regarded by many as a display of arrogance by a super-power, a nation that seems slow or unwilling to learn important lessons from its own failed and questionable interventions in countries such as Iran, Chile, Vietnam, Haiti, and Panama.

I believe it is possible to gain the good will and friendship of people in client countries. It certainly would help if foreign aid projects were carefully conceptualized, and staffed with qualified people to implement them. Education projects, for example, need to be carefully planned to dovetail with the current level of technology in the client country. Local participation in the initiation and implementation of projects would certainly help in developing sustainable programs that can continue even after the technicians of the donor country have left. And to insure that the projects are on track, they must be monitored every step of the way. Internal evaluations of foreign aid projects appear to be less objective than assessments by external organizations. External evaluators tend to be more honest and less forgiving. Without a rigorous and honest assessment, I believe we risk repeating poorly conceived foreign aid missions from one country to the next.

But opportunity to work overseas need not be discouraging; it can be fun and exciting, both professionally and socially. There is not much one can do about how the United States government decides to spend taxpayers' money overseas, or how universities make decisions picking people to run international projects, and much less about the mental faculties and limited experience of a project leader. So if you are involved in such projects, be your own boss to the extent you can. Get to know the local people and travel, always remembering to look out for your own safety. Find ways to enrich your experience overseas. There will be lighter moments that can lessen the drudgery of poorly conceptualized assignments.

The project in Swaziland was designed to help reform the elementary school curriculum to reflect more of the country's indigenous culture and its aspirations as an independent nation, and less of the influence of British colonialism. The project was sub-divided into different components, including Language Arts, Social Studies, Science, Mathematics, and Teacher Education. I was in charge of the teacher education component. This provided in-service training for teachers for the new materials produced by our project. It was another multi-million dollar undertaking funded by the United States Agency for International Development and administered by Eastern Michigan University.

I should mention that my local counterparts in Swaziland, as well as in North Yemen, viewed me as a colleague from another third world country. This resulted in a closer working relationship with them than what they afforded the White team members of our project. I was invited to their homes for dinner, asked to join them for a drink in Swaziland and included to chew *qat* (a mild narcotic) in Yemen. These occasions encouraged informality and exchange of ideas. It was at these settings that they sometimes suggested ways that they could facilitate approval of something in which I might have been interested at the time.

A good example was the approval of my proposal, which I called "Mobile Teachers Center" (MTC), to provide in-service training for teachers in the rural areas of Swaziland. I thought the MTC was a sensible idea for a country where most of the teachers worked in rural areas and transportation to the towns was not readily available to the teachers. For some reason, the American project leader and his Swazi counterpart were indifferent to the idea. Thus, getting the MTC approved eventually required making use of my special relationship with our other counterparts from the client country. I decided to discuss my proposal informally with the Minister of Education and his Permanent Secretary (PS), just to learn their thinking. They were enthusiastic about the concept of an MTC. Their approval was assured. They suggested, however, that we go through the formality of asking the American project leader and the Swazi Director to meet with the PS to "discuss" what their thinking was about my proposal. The Minister of Education and the PS were already aware that the American project leader and his Swazi counterpart were indifferent to the idea of a Mobile Teacher Center.

As prearranged between the PS and myself, the PS asked me to outline my proposal as the group convened in his office later that week. While I gave my presentation, the PS conspicuously made approving gestures and comments, as if he was hearing my proposal for the first time! After my brief talk, the PS asked the American project leader and Swazi Director what they thought about the MTC proposal. To my surprise they gave their enthusiastic agreement and praises for a "great concept!" They must have noticed the approving gestures of the PS during my presentation. So the two reluctant and bewildered project administrators thought it more prudent to endorse the proposal! I speculated that on their drive back from Mbabane to Manzini, the American project leader and Swazi Director probably wondered what had hit them!

After a nationally televised introduction of the Mobile Teacher Center at a government building provided by the PS, the MTC was well-received by parents and teachers. The United States Ambassador attended, as did members of the Ministry of Education, and some representatives of other foreign aid missions. The event was not only televised, it was also covered on the front page of the *Swazi Times*, including pictures of the United States Ambassador looking at our exhibits of teaching aids made out of throw-away and/or inexpensive materials. This well-publicized introduction was calculated (1) to dramatize its approval by the Ministry of Education, (2) to insure that the teachers would be receptive to the idea, and (3) to encourage the education inspectors to be cooperative. A few months later, a delegation from the Ministry of Education of Zambia came to Swaziland to visit our education project. It was a bit of a let down for the Swazi director, who had proudly greeted them, after they told him they had come to see me to learn more about the Mobile Teacher Center!

After completing in 1981 my two-year assignment in Swaziland, I was appointed in 1984 as "Chief of Party" for a United States Agency for International Development foreign aid project in North Yemen, administered by Eastern Michigan University. Incidentally, my selection as head of the project in North Yemen was the result of the intervention by the Yemeni Director of Education of the government of Yemen. He selected me over the person recommended by Eastern Michigan University. The Yemeni Director of Education asked me later what was the rationale that made Eastern Michigan University recommend someone who the Yemeni Director thought was clearly less qualified than me, based on his comparison of our credentials. Since I did not want to pursue what I considered an unpleasant personal experience, I jokingly replied that it was sometimes extremely difficult to understand the ways of the university. Not wanting to drop the matter so easily, he reminded me that the person selected by Eastern Michigan University was White, and he was from a university other than the base of the project! He ended his inquiry with a slight shake of his head, obviously bothered by what he called an example of "racism and discrimination" by an American university. The ranking of the two candidates by Eastern Michigan University was later confirmed to me by the university's messenger, who personally brought the two sets of credentials, mine and EMU's preferred candidate's, to Yemen.

While in Yemen, I had informal visits by officials of the Ministry of Education. A huge world map hung on the wall of my office. While chatting with me, they would casually look at my map. They did not say anything about the map until their second visit, about a week later. In a somewhat light-hearted manner, one of them commented that my map was not accurate. It had Israel on it, and he noted that "Legally, Israel does not exist." I commented that I had not given that much thought, and left it at that. The following week when they came for their visit, one of them went straight to the map. When he joined us later, while we were drinking the usual hospitality hot sweetened tea, he proudly announced that he just "helped" me. He had brought a piece of paper and Scotch tape and covered Israel! "Now," he assured me, "you are not going to be in trouble with other visitors!" With another year and a half to go for my assignment, prudence suggested that I leave the scotch tape intact on the map!

The outcome of another incident was entirely different. One afternoon when I had my weekly visit with the Director of Education who had selected me as head of the multi-million dollar education project, he called my attention to his suspicion that my Administrative Assistant was an "Israeli spy." It was an accusation that I was entirely unprepared for. I looked at my translator and suggested that he ask the Director to repeat what he had said to be sure I understood him accurately. The Director repeated the same thing that I heard the first time! He added that unless I fired the employee in question, the government of Yemen had no desire to continue the project! I replied politely that my Administrative Assistant was not an Israeli spy and that I was not even aware of his religious affiliation. What was important to me, I emphasized, was that he performed his responsibilities as a good

Administrative Assistant.

I looked at the clock on the wall; it was getting close to three o'clock. I calculated I had time to go to the USAID office in Sanaa and discuss the matter with the Director of USAID and his education officer. On the way to the car, I checked with my translator, Hassan, if there was any chance that he had misunderstood the Yemeni Director. Hassan was emphatic that the Director was very clear.

The Director of USAID and the Education Officer were supportive of my interpretation and suggestion that the Yemeni Director was probably bluffing, and that we should take a stand in supporting my Administrative Assistant. Assured of their support, Hassan drove me back to the Ministry since there was time left for the Yemeni Director to see me. I began by indicating that I had looked forward to completing my tenure in Yemen. Unfortunately, the USAID had taken the view that we would rather discontinue the project than fire one of our employees based on no more than the allegation that he was a spy. Frankly, I had my fingers crossed as I made my pitch because my position was based on the assumption that the Director was bluffing and that Yemen could not afford to give up a multi-million dollar project. I think he was surprised that I had gone to the USAID for consultation. The Director was quiet and then he said that he had been misunderstood. It was his way out and I closed the matter at that point by indicating I was glad it was just a misunderstanding. On our way to the car, Hassan was understandably furious. "Dr. Samonte, he was very clear with what he said. And he even repeated it when you asked him!" I reassured Hassan I had confidence in his translation, but we had to give the Yemeni Director a reasonable way out. I am sure the Director realized that the Yemeni Minister of Education would have given him hell for risking a multi-million dollar project. My Administrative Assistant stayed on and I never told him about that session at the Ministry of Education.

The Yemeni Director and I worked well together for the duration of my stay. He even requested that I do a survey of schools, allowing me to select my own sample, and identify their strengths and weaknesses. I did just that, much to the surprise of the USAID office, which informed me that two American educators who had wanted to carry out a similar survey were refused by the Director. The two researchers were later asked to leave the country! Obviously, the Director of Education continued to have confidence in me, in spite of my stand against him when I supported my Administrative Assistant.

I cannot forget the other workers who helped me a great deal in connection with the project in North Yemen. I had translators, drivers, and one I will call my "special fixer." Ibrahim, one of four drivers, used to bring clusters of freshly harvested dates to the apartment when Judy was visiting from the United States. He must have remembered, too, my story about one of my trips to the seaport of Hodeida when I could not get fresh fish at a seaside restaurant. The waiter had assured me he had something even better, "imported canned sardines from Portugal!" During one of my subsequent trips to Hodeida with Judy, Ibrahim knocked at our hotel door one evening to surprise us with delicious grilled fish that was still hot. He had bought it at the public market.

They did have fresh fish in Hodeida!

Sadek was another driver with the project. When I found out that four of the seven vehicles no longer had insurance coverage, I had them impounded until all insurance papers were in order. Sadek came to my office and politely assured me not to worry about insurance papers. He said "Allah will take care." I thanked him for his concern, but I also indicated that since I was not Muslim, I was not sure if I was protected by Allah.

Sadek drove me home one day and confided that his wife had been vomiting in the morning. I suggested the possibility that she might be pregnant. "It cannot be. I already have eight children!" he countered. A couple of days later, as we were walking across the parking lot, he got closer to me and he looked around to be sure nobody was listening. He said, in a whisper, that he had special medicine for his wife. I was puzzled by all the secrecy. Looking around some more, he took something from his pocket that he called "special medicine from Israel." There in his cupped hand was a small bottle of *Alka Seltzer*! A week later, I asked how the special medicine from Israel was working. He was quiet for a while, which got me a little worried, and then he said his wife was pregnant again!

For all his family concerns, he came to see me during my last week in Yemen. He said, "You stay, Dr. Samonte. You, Director of Education of Yemen. You fix bad project when you come. You finished quickly." I thanked him for his confidence. After Sadek left my office, I must confess I felt a bit elated to think one of the Yemenis I worked with felt that way. I chuckled, too, when I recalled that it was Sadek who joked about "driving for Dr. Samonte was like Ramadan," for I did not allow smoking or drinking in the car when I was a passenger. Later on during my tenure in Yemen, I did allow the driver to chew *qat* when I was a passenger and we were on long trips since the driver informed me chewing *qat* helped him to stay awake!

Hassan was in a class by himself. He was my personal driver, translator and my "special fixer." He could get shipments for the project released from the Bureau of Customs in one or two days. That was quite an achievement if you consider how other projects struggled with that problem. The Chief of Party of one of the American projects mentioned that he counted 48 signatures and waited another three weeks before one of his shipments was released. He asked me how long it took to get my shipments. I just said "It takes time." I did not want to reveal my secret. Evidently it was a secret I could not conceal indefinitely for, one day, I received a call from a friend at the USAID office. He asked delicately if I "could lend Hassan to their office even just for a few days?"

Hassan was always protective of me. He made sure I did not drive if it could be avoided. He knew that if I ever got into a car accident, the foreigner was always at fault, with all kinds of unpleasant consequences. He was also concerned about my housekeeping chores. Since I was in Yemen by myself, living in a huge four-bedroom luxury apartment, in a complex built especially for the families of members of the diplomatic corps and foreign business representatives, he suggested it would not be a bad idea if I had a "young live-in maid from Ethiopia!" His attractive wife was from Ethiopia, and their house was usually a gathering place for a handful of Ethiopian refugees for Sunday dinner. Three or four young Ethiopian women were invited regularly for these Sunday dinners. The women were nice-looking, and I did not miss that. I could not help but smile at the thought that Hassan was an incurable fixer indeed, always looking out for my well-being.

Exploring Distant Shores

When I decided to go to the Kingdom of Swaziland, as Adviser to its Ministry of Education, one of my colleagues asked, somewhat facetiously, "Where in hell is Swaziland anyway?" I responded, "I do not know, but I am going anyway." Actually the country where I was being assigned, under a USAID contract with Eastern Michigan University, is a tiny country, about 6,704 square miles and almost totally surrounded by South Africa, except for a short common border with Mozambique. At the time of my assignment, it had a population of about 500,000. When I realized how small and remote it appeared on the map, I said to Judy, half-jokingly, that I was finally about to be assigned to a country where I would probably not find any other Filipinos.

The Philippine Overseas Employment Administration reported that for 2000–2001, there were approximately 866,590 Filipinos who were classified as "Overseas

Workers." These were distributed in various regions of the world, with 297,533 in the Middle East, 285,051 in Asia, 43,019 in Europe, 10,679 in the "Americas," 4,679 in Africa, 6,823 in the Trust Territories, 2,061 in Oceania, and 11,530 "Unspecified." These workers included laborers, domestics, and professionals like accountants, engineers, nurses and physicians. The pressure for Filipinos to work overseas is due to many factors. These include a rapidly growing population in the Philippines, a rate of about 25% of the population living in poverty, as reported by the World Bank in 2000; having a high percentage of Filipinos who have earned college degrees without a corresponding increase in opportunities for employment in the Philippines; a sluggish economy that has not kept up with more energetic nations like Taiwan, Singapore, South Korea, or Thailand; and a government that has been saddled with corruption, a problem that does not show any sign of abating.

Even with the extensive distribution of overseas workers, I was not expecting to find Filipinos in Swaziland. But there they were! It was a nice surprise when I was informed by my local counterparts that there were indeed Filipino workers in the country, and it was even more pleasant to discover that they were regarded in high esteem by the Swazis. I was told that the architect who helped design the palace of King Sobhuza II of Swaziland was a Filipino and so were the engineers that helped to maintain it. All three physicians of Nazarene hospital, located in Manzini, were Filipinos, and so was an instructor at the University of Swaziland. I spent some enjoyable time with them as they made sure I was invited to their parties and tennis games at the courts of Nazarene Hospital. The medical doctors were always there for anything I needed, such as an inoculation required when I had field trips from the middle *veld* to the low *veld*.

As a surprise for Judy when she came for a short stay in Swaziland, I arranged a vacation to the spectacular Victoria Falls in Zimbabwe. While we were in Zimbabwe, we had another pleasant experience when we were visited by a Filipino who was one of the supervisors of the hotel where we stayed in Harare.

The reputation of (North) Yemen as a country that can be a difficult place to work for women who were raised in a more liberal setting that recognized greater equality between genders, has apparently not deterred Filipinos from applying for work in that country. Most of the nurses were Filipinos in two hospitals in Sanaa, the capital of Yemen, where I lived for the duration of my assignment in that country. The head of the United Nations' office for refugees was also a Filipino. In addition to the professionals, there were Filipinos who worked as housemaids in private homes, as room cleaners in the hotels, and as chefs and cooks for the luxury hotels.

But there was another surprise for me. When I reported for my first day of work, the clerical secretary of the project was another Filipino. Unfortunately, after a few months on the project, I faced the painful and difficult decision of firing her. She had made the mistake of telling me that she was making extra money by selling liquor in the black market.

In Yemen, the sale of liquor in the black market was forbidden by law. But members of the diplomatic corps and foreign aid missions were allowed to buy alcoholic beverages at their respective commissaries, at a nominal price, up to each individual's authorized monthly quota. The United States Ambassador found it necessary to occasionally remind members of the United States mission that any American found selling alcohol on the black market would be put on the next available plane for home. It was within this context that I could not allow my Filipino secretary to be associated with a multi-million United States foreign aid project while she was engaged in the black market. It was a painful decision for me because I knew what Filipino workers went through to find work and maintain employment overseas.

Unfortunately, with the large number of Filipino workers overseas, there have been allegations of crime, some leading to convictions, imprisonment and even executions. But there were also widespread abuses suffered by overseas workers. These include unscrupulous recruiters who exploit eager applicants by demanding exorbitant fees, contracts that are not honored by employers, and working conditions that sometimes include physical and sexual abuses. Compounding these problems is the Philippine government that is apparently only too eager to lay its hands on remitted dollars, but is unable to provide adequate protection for Filipino overseas workers.

On a more personal level, when I was in England to accompany some American students for a course at the University of Reading one summer in the early 1970s, two

Filipino workers came to see me. They introduced themselves as representatives of Filipino overseas workers in the area. These included mostly domestic workers, and they complained about the conditions of work, salaries, and other terms of contracts that had not been honored by their employers. Desperate for help, they came to see me when they learned that a Filipino was in charge of a summer program at the University of Reading. I explained to them that I was not in an official capacity to help, but I would review their concerns and explore some possible options with them. I suggested that they should list the important problems and document them. Then they should select a spokesman or two, go to the Philippine Embassy in London, and present their documented grievances to the proper office of the Embassy. I also suggested that they ask the Official when the workers could expect a reply and what specific actions the Embassy planned to take.

I was confronted with a comparable situation in 1984 in Sanaa, North Yemen, when some Filipino nurses came to see me to complain about certain provisions of their contracts that had not been honored. Not having any Philippine Embassy or Consulate in Yemen made it much more difficult for them to request assistance from the Philippine government. The nurses informed me that the nearest office of the Philippine Department of Foreign Affairs was in Saudi Arabia. They had petitioned the office in Saudi Arabia, and a Filipino official had made a token visit to Yemen, but nothing more ever happened. Attempts by the nurses to organize in Sanaa only resulted in more repressive measures for the organizers. They were told they would be deported at the nurses' expense if they continued to demand improvement of the nurses' working conditions. The inability of the Philippine government to protect its overseas workers abroad is a continuing problem that seems no closer to being resolved.

Let me move on to a more upbeat occasion. Back at the Sheraton Hotel of Sanaa, when the Filipino chef and his cooks heard that a Filipino was in charge of a United States foreign aid project, they suggested they could come to my apartment on their day off, to cook for me and some invited guests for dinner. They added that they would wear their uniforms and told me to introduce them as my cooks to impress the visitors. They did just that. The chef and two cooks came complete with their white aprons and tall white chefs hats. I invited the Director of the USAID mission in Yemen and his wife, and the Education Officer and his wife, for dinner. From before-dinner drinks, appetizers, dinner, dessert to after-dinner drinks, those compatriots put on quite a show while my visitors kept looking at them and then at me. Speechless for a while, the Director finally leaned over and asked in a whisper, "Who are these guys, anyway?" Without hesitation, I told him that they were members of the kitchen staff, including the chef, of the Sheraton! The Director had to digest that one for a while. After recovering, he asked "What are they doing here?" Without missing a beat, I simply said, "They cook for me on their day off!" After my no-big-deal expression, it was my turn to be surprised when it was time for the chef and his two cooks to return to the Sheraton. We were having our after-dinner coffee when they came forward and politely announced that it was time for them to go. They then asked me, to further impress my guests, what I wanted to be prepared for next time. I was not prepared for that one, but I maintained my composure. I played the game along with the cooks, and told them I would give the next menu some thought and I would let them know in good time. If only I had a hidden camera, I would have thoroughly enjoyed reviewing my guests' expressions as they tried to figure out "Filipino culture" and/or their new Chief of Party from the Philippines, who was just another overseas worker anyway!

There was another occasion when some Filipino engineers really came through for me in meeting a tight deadline. One of the sub-sections of my project in Yemen was the installation of a complete Audio-Visual Center at the University of Sanaa. Because equipment had to be compatible with broadcasting frequencies in the Middle East, I requested authorization from USAID Washington to purchase all needed equipment from a business company in Saudi Arabia. This meant that electronic and electrical engineers had to accompany the equipment for installation.

When the four engineers arrived, they all turned out to be Filipinos. This resulted in some kidding from the USAID education officer, who joked that I was engaged in a bit of nepotism! Actually, when I talked to the owner of the company, he said his first preference was to hire Arabic-speaking engineers. Consequently, he interviewed some 3,000 applicants, mostly from Egypt. Unfortunately, he said, not a single one of them met his technical requirements. Next, he went to the Philippines to size up the pool of applicants. He said he needed to interview only twelve applicants to find the six engineers he needed! So there they were in Yemen; I was pleased and I was not disappointed by their work.

The challenge was that barely a month was left before the start of Ramadan and that was all the time I had to complete and close the project. The Yemeni government was to have everything ready; this included tearing down some concrete partitions, digging for the placement of cables, and attaching all the necessary electrical connections. None of those requirements were done in spite of repeated requests from my office. When the engineers saw this, they were a bit shocked, to say the least. They asked me, “When do you need this completed, Doc?” I explained my predicament with the tight schedule that the Yemeni government had given me. After carefully surveying the situation, they came to see me. “We’ll finish it for you, Doc!” Did they ever work! They assumed other duties like digging, knocking down a concrete wall, and working late into the night to install electrical cables. They finished before Ramadan started and they did a fine job. This prompted Dr. Al-Khader, Dean of the College of Education, Sanaa University, to express his admiration. “Ric, I have never seen a group that worked as hard and as efficiently as these Filipino engineers!” Al-Khader was not going to let it end right there. “Ric”, he said, “before you leave Yemen, I would like to open this Audio Visual Center properly. We have overcome all the problems and in a very fine way.” I thanked him and asked what he had in mind. "I'll ask the Prime Minister of North Yemen to open the facilities, invite members of the diplomatic corps to attend, and the unavoidable soldiers will be deployed for security." That he did, and we completed the project and opened the AV center in fine style. The United States Ambassador came over to me, offered a hearty handshake, and said "You can hold your head high, it's a job well done!"

Epilogue

White Dove

Some old beliefs are difficult to forget, and contemporary events can sometimes trigger the revival of latent memories. When I returned to the Philippines in 1998 to attend Father's funeral, it was also an occasion to visit relatives and classmates from the high school. Seeing old friends again always made the long and tiring flight from Detroit to Manila worthwhile. But attending Dad's funeral was also an occasion to "revisit" or should I say to be "revisited" by ghost stories from my childhood days, and it was amusing to hear about them again.

The spirit of the departed do come back, so they said. On All Souls' Night at the stroke of midnight, children were alert to the howling of the dogs for they believed that it was an unmistakable sign that the spirits were back. The dogs, we were told, could see what we ordinary mortals could not see. The spirit of the dead came back to reciprocate the thoughtfulness of relatives who cleaned the tombstones, decorated with fresh cut flowers, lighted candles and visited with other families. The cemetery on All Souls' Day was a place for merriment with strings of colored lights, food and socializing with friends.

Back in town, it was not only the baying of dogs and the far-reaching sound of the *campana* (bell of the church tower) at twelve midnight that proclaimed that the spirits were back in town. There were other signs: the smell of burning candle and the strong perfume that seemed to come from nowhere. To be on the safe side, we prepared offerings for the "visitors" like homemade cakes arranged between two candles in front of some religious pictures. The best sign that the spirits were sampling the offerings was the line of ants to and from the food. The spirits took all kinds of forms, we were told, including that faceless translucent image floating in the garden, that smell and, of course, the ants!

The morning following Father's cremation, I went downstairs to join my two sisters at the breakfast table. After the usual greeting, the two of them resumed their whispered conversation. I helped myself to a little bit of breakfast. My sisters continued their quiet conversation. I jokingly asked them what they seemed to be so secretive about. They looked at each other as if to say, "You tell him!" Francy hesitated. She finally said that they thought "Dad visited last night." How did they know, I asked. They claimed there were three loud knocks on their bedroom door and, when they opened it, there was no one there! They added, for good measure I assumed, that the wind chime in the garden was ringing like crazy and yet there was no breeze at all. I did not say anything for I did not want to make light of their earnest observations. The next day at breakfast, the two were again having a whispered conversation. "Dad visited again last night," said Francy. I already knew it because that time it was the "visitor from Ann Arbor" who knocked on their door at midnight, and I also knocked on a few more doors for good measure. I did not say anything.

The following night, around two or three a.m., I was awakened by a loud knock on the door of Dad and Mom's bedroom where I was then staying by myself. I was awakened and, before I could open the door, I distinctly heard Dad's voice say, "I am glad you came home." I stayed in bed, my heart pounding a bit. I tried to go back to sleep but I could not. I explained this to myself that given my emotional state at that time, I could have imagined hearing Dad's voice and left it at that.

More easy to explain was an amusing observation on my first day back at the house when Dad was still lying in state at the chapel of the University of the Philippines. I stood at the balcony outside his bedroom, just as Dad used to do. Like him, I was also dressed in short pants, T-shirt and a cap. I stood there and imagined what Dad could have looked at in the street in the mornings. The street was only about thirty feet from the second floor balcony. It was that time of the morning when people passed by on their way to work. One man was walking leisurely by himself swinging his brief case.

He happened to glance toward me, he did a double take and suddenly accelerated his pace without looking back! Since then, some people in the neighborhood still talk about "sightings" on that balcony.

But there are events that I do not want to understand too much in rational terms, like the grandeur of a colorful

sunrise or sunset, the beauty of a newly opened flower, or the magic of a moonlit night. My sister told me that Father ate at the dinning room by himself after Mother passed away. There was a large sliding glass door in the dinning room that opened into the garden, and he sometimes opened that door briefly for cross ventilation. My sister added that one day, just a few days before Father died, a white dove flew in through the opened door and perched on the back of what used to be Mother's chair. Father was apparently touched by the event, and he gently offered food to the dove that took it from his hand.

According to my sister, the dove visited a few more times going through the same routine of flying in, perching on Mother's chair, and taking the food from Father's hand. I thought there was a little bit of melo-drama there, but I did not say anything. One morning I was having breakfast by myself after my sisters had left for work. With Father gone, I sat at the head of the table where he usually sat. I opened the sliding door for a little ventilation, and a white dove flew in. It perched on Mother's chair long enough for me to take a couple of pictures, and then it flew away. It never came back again while I was there. A few days after my visit home, my sister wrote to me that the white dove came back accompanied by a gray one; they perched on a branch of a tree close to the dining room door. They came back a few more days after that and then flew away together never to be seen again.

Recipes

Recipes

The recipes included are simplified recollections of dishes I associate with some members of the family, and other people I have encountered in my assignments overseas. Reproducing them was limited by availability of ingredients, the need to simplify, and how accurately I could remember them. They probably would not pass the tests of culinary experts, but they did serve to satisfy my longings for some flavors remembered from way back. It is in the spirit of making do with what one has that I put these recipes together.

One time while I was in Yemen, I invited some friends over for dinner. Along with other Filipino dishes, I also prepared *pancit*, a noodle dish. One of the American guests commented, "Is this what you call *pancit*?" I was taken aback by the brashness of the question and the manner in which it was asked, but I politely responded that it was. She continued to tell me that she had Filipino friends in Hawaii and that the *pancit* they prepared was different. I reviewed in my mind what I might have given her to drink, and I also wondered why I invited her in the first place! At any rate, I explained patiently that the term *pancit*, as I understood it used in the Philippines, was a generic term. Thus, a dish called *pancit* could vary depending, for example, on the kind of noodle used, on the ingredients, and whether it is soupy like "*pancit mami*" or dry like *pancit guisado*. She just responded with "Oh." In this connection, it would be well to mention that the use of terms like *adobo, pinakbet, sinuman* or *kilawen* could refer to modified versions from one region to another in the Philippines.

Steamed Fish (from Mom)

This is a simplified version of the steamed fish recipe given to Mother by the vendor. Traditionally, two clay pots were used, one on top of the other like a double boiler. The lower pot would have contained water and the top part could have been an old pot with a hole at the bottom big enough to put your fist through. The hole would be covered with rice straw over which the fish would be arranged for steaming. Before steaming, the fish would have been marinated for an hour or two in vinegar with sliced or diced raw ginger, and salt to taste.

My version of the recipe uses a large stainless steel frying pan with green onion leaves laid across the bottom to keep the fish from sticking. You may marinate the fish if you wish, but it is not necessary with this modified version.

Ingredients: (for 2–4 people)

Filet of salmon, about 10 inches long, or about one pound.
Cut strips across filet 2 inches wide or wider. (When I use brook trout, I steam the fish whole, 1 fish per person.)
Raw ginger, half the size of your thumb, diced or sliced
2 tablespoons vinegar
Salt or soy sauce to taste
Green onion leaves

Spread onion leaves on the pan and put half of the ginger over the onion leaves. Arrange fish in a single layer on the onion leaves. Pour 2 tablespoons vinegar over the fish and scatter the rest of the ginger on top of the fish. Sprinkle salt or soy sauce to taste. Cover and simmer on medium heat. Check occasionally to be sure some liquid remains. There should be enough liquid from the vinegar and the fish. (If the liquid evaporates because you left the heat too high, just add 2 tablespoons of water). Cook about ten minutes; more time may be needed depending upon thickness of the fish. I like salmon filet at least an inch thick. If it is thinner than 1 inch, it tends to be drier. Other kinds of firm-fleshed fish I like for steaming are whitefish, brook trout (whole), filet of lake trout, mackerel (cut across whole fish in 4–5 inch segments), tuna and *tilapia*. Experiment with others to find your favorite taste and texture.

Serve with steamed rice, almost ripe mango (sliced and sprinkled with sugar if still a bit sour), a green salad and your favorite vegetable. It is also delicious served cold the following day.

Arroz Caldo (From Dad)

For many young boys in Laoag, part of growing up would include being out at night with the other boys in the neighborhood to cook *arroz caldo*. This is a thick soupy mixture of chicken and rice, flavored with other ingredients, like fresh ginger and squeezed cream of freshly grated coconut meat. When cooked, it has the consistency of oatmeal or cream of wheat. *Pancit* and *arroz caldo* were two of the dishes that Dad liked to prepare occasionally even as an adult.

Plans for an evening of cooking might be triggered by one of the boys informing the others that his folks would be away for a couple of days or so. That meant someone's house was available for an evening of camaraderie and cooking *arroz caldo*, *pancit* (noodles), or whatever available ingredients might dictate, like goat meat for *caldereta* (a goat stew with fancy ingredients).

The organization of the *arroz caldo* cooking event would start with decisions on who would bring chicken, rice, coconut, seasoning, etc. No questions were asked about where or how each one produced his contribution for the *arroz caldo*! The boy at whose house we cooked contributed the use of pots, plates, and other necessary equipment for dressing the live chicken. The kids who could not afford to contribute any of the ingredients usually offered to dress the chicken, cook, and clean up afterward. It was during activities like these that we learned how to cook *arroz caldo*, even just by watching, and so it was for me when I was old enough to be allowed to stay out later at night.

On one of these occasions, my good friend, Victor ("Toring") Pascual, informed us that his grandmother would be away for the weekend on a business trip, an unmistakable offer for a place to cook *arroz caldo*! Addong, an older boy from the neighborhood, volunteered to dress the chicken, to cook and to wash the pots and pans afterwards since he could not afford to contribute any of the ingredients. Erning, Romeo and I reduced *Lola* Sabina's flock of chickens by one, our contribution for that evening.

With a little light from the wood-burning clay stove and a candle on the kitchen table, we sat around chatting, laughing and having a good time. Meanwhile, Addong was seriously at work stirring the pot, tasting occasionally, and adding a little salt as needed. Sometimes he would add water from the *malabi* (a large clay pot containing water) that was next to the stove. Water was usually added to the *arroz caldo* while cooking, since it got thicker as the rice expanded. Framed against the flickering light from the stove, I thought Addong looked very much like the horror movie actor, Bela Lugosi. Addong did not pay much attention to our funny stories, he seemed engrossed with his cooking. To him it was an evening of good eating. It was then I decided to check the water in the *malabi* with *Mama* Ti's flash light! "Yikes!" I exclaimed. "The water is full of cockroaches!" I expected that would have caught the attention of Addong. Not a bit, he went on stirring the pot with that Bela Lugosi look and kept tasting the *arroz caldo*. Even if Addong ended up eating the *arroz caldo* all by himself, every one had a good time that evening.

When traditionally prepared, the ingredients of *arroz caldo* included the whole dressed chicken, cream from a freshly grated coconut, a tiny bit of lard, salt and raw ginger. It was served with diced and browned garlic sprinkled on top of each serving, and sometimes with Chinese pickled radishes as a side dish. My version, by comparison, is highly simplified. But I can assure you it still reminds me of those memorable evenings with the neighborhood kids when we experimented with the preparation of *arroz caldo*.

Ingredients: (for 4 people)

2 Chicken thighs (or a left-over turkey thigh)

1 cup rice, uncooked (I prefer long grain, which does not get as mushy as short grain rice, but either may be used)

1 (49 oz.) can of low fat, low sodium chicken broth, no MSG (or 3 (14 oz.) cans)

1 teaspoon of vegetable oil (optional)

1/3 teaspoon onion powder

Salt to taste (I find that there is enough salt in the broth for my taste, so experiment first without adding salt. You can always sprinkle a little soy sauce in when you eat it.)

Ginger, half the size of your thumb, thinly sliced

Heat the cooking oil in the pan. Sauté chicken thighs (slight browning brings out more flavor from the chicken). Sprinkle onion powder on chicken as it starts to brown. As the onion powder begins to slightly brown, add the broth quickly to prevent the onion powder from turning dark and bitter! Add one cup of uncooked rice and ginger. Simmer for 45–60 minutes. Stir occasionally to keep the rice from sticking to the bottom of the pan. If you find that it is getting too thick, add a bit of water or broth as needed. When the chicken is almost cooked, you can poke the thigh with a ladle to separate the flesh from the bone. To avoid this process, you could cut the thigh meat into smaller pieces before you sauté it. I find it more convenient to just toss the two thighs into the pan.

Arroz caldo is sometimes served after midnight Mass on Christmas Eve, at midnight after greeting the New Year, or at any other time. I also like it for breakfast if there is some leftover.

French Toast (from Tio Papa)

Some of the middle-class Filipinos who went to the United States in the 1920s learned to cook, either through working in restaurants and/or cooking for themselves, since they did not have the luxury of having maids as they did back home in the Philippines. When *Tio Papa* returned to the Philippines after finishing his medical degree, he sometimes prepared pancakes, muffins, or French toast. These were skills that, I am sure, he did not have before he left the Philippines for the U.S. in 1921. The following is my version of Uncle Damaso's French toast. I make it using left-over bread. Any kind of bread works, but I prefer Italian bread or French baguette, for small-sized French toast.

Ingredients: (for 2 people)
4 slices of small palm-sized bread or 8 slices of baguette (3/4 inch thick)
1 egg (or 1/4 cup Egg Beaters)
1/2 cup of milk (whole, skim, non fat or soy milk)
1 teaspoon sugar (optional)
Sprinkle of cinnamon
vegetable oil

Combine eggs, milk, sugar, cinnamon and mix thoroughly. Place each slice into the mixture. Make sure not to saturate the slices of bread for that makes them soggy. On a pre-heated pan (medium heat), add a tiny bit of vegetable oil. Allow oil to get warm. Place the slices on the pan carefully as the soaked bread will easily fall apart. Covering the pan will provide more heat; turn the slices over to cook other side. Make sure each slice is cooked thoroughly. I like maple syrup and butter on my French toast. You could use jam or jelly if you prefer, or garnish with fresh berries and sprinkle with powdered sugar.

Fish Head Soup (from Lola Leoncia)

Since we lived on the first floor of the Segundo house during the early years of Mom and Dad's marriage, sometimes *Lola* Leoncia came downstairs to tell me she was making *lomo lomo* for breakfast, or fish head soup for lunch. I always found that invitation difficult to resist. In addition to being an active civic leader, *Lola* Leoncia was quite an accomplished cook. I have included in this book a modified version of her fish head soup, *lomo lomo* and her *Arroz Valenciana.* I do not know what kind of fish she used for her fish head soup. I remember it as a relatively large head that she cut into sections. The best I could find in Michigan was lake trout head, which is big enough (and I could get them free at Thill's Fisheries in Marquette!) If you do not wish to use fish heads, substitute one pound of salmon filet, cut into 2 to 3-inch chunks.

Ingredients: (for 2–4 people)

2–3 trout heads (each about the size of your fist)

1 large tomato, diced

1 medium onion, diced

ginger, half the size of your thumb, diced or sliced

Juice of one quarter of a lemon (instead of *tamarind* or *pias* which *Lola* used)

2 (14 oz.) cans of chicken broth (low fat, low sodium, no MSG)

Fresh spinach, one third of a 10 oz. bag (instead of *ampalaya* or *marunggay*)

1 teaspoon vegetable oil

Put vegetable oil in the cooking pan. Sauté onions, tomatoes and ginger. Add chicken broth. Simmer for 5 minutes to allow the flavors to mix. Add fish heads and simmer for about 10 minutes. Add spinach and lemon juice 5 minutes before soup is finished cooking.

Lomo Lomo (from Lola Leoncia)

Lomo lomo was usually prepared for breakfast and served with steamed rice, but it can be served at any meal. Not knowing then what the dish was called, I coined "*cot-cotsay*" as my special name for it. Chives (*cotsay* in Ilocano) was, to me, one of *lomo lomo's* unique and conspicuous ingredients since, it stayed green if it was not cooked too long. Judy has a good crop of chives planted in her flower garden in our backyard in Ann Arbor. She started it from one plant, and since it has grown luxuriantly, she has subdivided it a number of times to be planted elsewhere in her garden or to be shared with friends. We have more chives than we need for *lomo lomo* throughout Spring, Summer and Fall. Its violet flowers are quite decorative during Spring. *Lola* also had her own chives which she grew in flower pots on the *asotea* of the Segundo house. Since we have a year-round growing period in the Philippines, *Lola* Leoncia was well supplied with the special ingredient for one of my favorite dishes.

Ingredients: (for 2–4 people)

8–16 oz. of pork (loin, chops, or whatever you have including chicken)

2 cloves of garlic

Raw ginger, half the size of your thumb, sliced or diced

Ground pepper and salt to taste

"Patis" fish sauce, instead of salt (optional)

Fresh chives, one half cup, chopped in 1 inch long pieces

2 (14 oz.) cans chicken broth (low fat, low sodium if you prefer

no MSG), you can also use plain water (I think chicken broth gives it more flavor)

Cut meat into strips 1/2 inch thick, 1/2 inch wide, 2 inches long. Put a small amount of vegetable oil on cooking pan. Sauté meat. Add diced garlic when meat starts to brown and allow garlic to brown. Add raw ginger. Allow flavors to blend and then add chicken broth. Add 1/2 teaspoon of patis if you wish (only for those used to fish sauce or those who are adventurous) and simmer for about 30 minutes or until meat is tender. Add chives a few minutes before serving . Serve with steamed rice.

Paella (from Lola Leoncia)

I would not be able to list all the ingredients that *Lola* Leoncia included whenever she prepared *Arroz Valenciana*. I do remember that it was yellow, had chicken, ham, chorizos and green peas among other things. More important to me was that I liked it very much. It is said that traditionally, *paella* was cooked outdoors over an open fire by picnickers in Spain. During a few trips to Spain for vacations in the 1960s when I was teaching in England, my family sampled *paella* in different restaurants in Barcelona, Madrid and Segovia. There were variations, as expected, from one restaurant to another, but the affinity between the *paella* we sampled in Spain and what *Lola* Leoncia prepared was definitely there! Here is my simplified version.

Ingredients: (for 4–8 people)
4–6 pieces chicken thighs (or 1 whole small frying chicken)
12 medium to large shrimps
1 pepperoni (regular hot-dog size)
1 cup diced onion
1 cup diced tomatoes (or canned)
1 cup diced bell pepper
1 small bottle of pimento
2 cloves of garlic
1 tablespoon of vegetable oil or olive oil
1 cup frozen green peas
Any left over meat, like ham or roast pork
A pinch of saffron (add a few drops of yellow food coloring, if small amount of expensive saffron does not color the rice adequately)
2 cups rice, uncooked
3 cups chicken broth

1 (6 oz.) can of minced clams (it has almost a cup of liquid which adds up to 4 cups of liquid with the 3 cups of chicken broth)
Salt and pepper to taste

Heat 1 tablespoon of olive oil (or other vegetable oil) in a large frying pan and brown chicken thighs. Remove chicken from pan after about 20 minutes and set aside. Remove some of the oil from the pan if too much oil accumulated from the chicken, leave about a tablespoon of oil in the pan. Using the same pan, sauté crushed garlic. Add diced onions, diced or crushed tomatoes, and pimento. When the onions turn translucent, add 2 cups of uncooked rice into the mixture. Stir rice until it is fully coated with oil, add 3 cups of chicken broth and entire contents of 1 can minced clams. Add a pinch of saffron. Allow to boil briefly, then turn down heat and simmer. Add the chicken thighs, partially submerged in the rice, and any leftover meat you want to add, like ham or pork roast, cut in large 2 inch chunks. Cover the pieces of meat partially with rice to allow the flavor to blend with the rest of the ingredients. Do not cover the pan as long as heat is low. Cook over low heat until rice is tender, about 30–40 minutes. In a separate pan, fry shrimps and set aside to drain. Use the same shrimp pan to sauté sliced pepperoni and set aside to drain. Pour boiling water over 1 cup of frozen green peas, simmer for just 1 minute so peas do not over-cook! For presentation, put *paella* on a large platter and arrange shrimps, pepperoni and green peas on top.

You can make the *paella* as elaborate as you want depending upon what you have available and/or what you wish to spend on additions, like lobster, mussels, clams, scallops, fish, etc. My preference is to keep it simple, and be able to spend more time with guests and enjoy the evening.

Tapa (from tenant farmers)

Preserving meat or fish in the tropics is a challenge when there is no refrigeration. A number of traditional solutions include (1) not having any left-over meat or fish, (2) boiling it, (3) salting it heavily, or (4) drying it in the sun. Leaving no left-overs is not always practical as it depends upon how much food or fresh meat or fish there is to deal with. Boiling meat or steaming fish will preserve it for a few days. Salting heavily makes it last longer, and in some cases, like *bogoong* (salted fish sauce), it can last for months if done properly. Probably the most common method of preserving in the Philippines is to make use of the tropical sun, especially during the dry season. Drying filleted meat or large fish in the sun is convenient, and the process also seems to impart a special flavor. In our part of the Philippines, Ilocos Norte, the dried meat is called *tapa*. Sometimes laborers would bring a little piece of *tapa*, a tomato, and some cooked rice for their lunch.

During the war, I remember Father and I joined our tenant farmers for a hunt in the mountains. Since the Segundo farm in Surate, Dingras, was right at the base of the Cordillera, it was just a matter of climbing up from the base. We started hiking before sunrise and reached the hunting ground by mid-morning.

On one of those hunts, there must have been at least thirty of us, including the tenant farmers and their sons, my father and myself. I was fourteen years old; a few of the other boys were about my age and some slightly younger. Since there were no guns available to most civilians during the war, we had sharpened bamboo that we used as spears, *bolos* (broad heavy knives), and a long trap that looked to me like a tennis net, but was three times as high and as long as the narrow opening at the bottom of the ravine.

The hunting party was divided into four groups of about six to eight people each. Group A waited in line on top of a mountain ridge with Group B on another ridge facing Group A. Spanning between the two ridges, Group C was located perpendicular to Groups A and B. Below, at the narrow end of the small valley formed by the two ridges, Group D was stationed just outside the long net that was stretched at the base of the two ridges. At a given signal, Groups A, B, and C started the loudest racket they could make with shouts, banging cans, and dogs barking. While the noise-making was going on, Groups A, B and C converged towards the net. Group D remained quiet and waited for the wild animals to run towards the net. As soon as the animals got entangled in the net, the men in Group D who had the sharpened bamboos approached the animals for the kill. This process was repeated, after a lunch break, in three different locations.

For lunch for the two of us, Father brought rice, hard-boiled eggs, some ripe tomatoes, and salt. We situated ourselves on the forest floor next to a mountain stream. Some of us sat on large rocks. When the tenant farmer who was close by noticed that Father had brought some salt, he whispered to Father that he should not let the others see the salt for they thought it brings bad luck! Should we not catch anything or should some accident befall any member of the hunting party, Father might be blamed for it for bringing the salt. Father thanked the farmer, and he cautioned me to be careful not to mention it and not to be conspicuous using the salt. As it turned out, by mid-afternoon, we had captured four wild boar and one deer. It was a good hunt.

After the hunt, the men built a fire near the mountain stream. The tough hairs on the back of the wild boar were removed after pouring boiling water and before the gutted animals were laid on the fire. These long tough bristles from the back of the wild boar were used as needles by the men who made saddles or sheaths for *bolos*. The animals were then turned regularly over the fire and their remaining hair was efficiently scraped off with strips of bamboo. The meat was expertly divided with equal portions given to all, regardless of age. Each portion was wrapped in banana leaf, and each member carried his own share of the hunt. Father and I got our two portions. I felt immensely proud.

We started our walk back to the village while the sun was still up. As we approached the village below, there was still light. I could see and hear the women and children excitedly announce that we had been successful. We entered the village as triumphant hunters. I walked proudly with the group as I carried my share of the hunt. There was meat for the village, and all the women were happy, including Mother. You could hear happy chattering from the *nipa* huts into the night, and it was not long before smoke and the aroma of grilled meat started coming from the different kitchens.

The following day, you could see all the *nipa* huts in the village surrounded by thinly sliced meat hanging from bamboo poles. The hot tropical sun sterilized and dried the meat, and the poles were high enough to keep the meat safe from the dogs. The *tapa* dried under the sun for several days before it was stored safely, ready for use for many days after that.

Because *tapa* is made to be stored, it is prepared when there is more fresh meat or fish than can be consumed in one or two meals. Thus, the proportions suggested below are for more than one meal. The quality of the meat could include cheaper cuts like chuck or round steak since they are cut into slices no more than a centimeter thick, even thinner if you can (partial freezing aids slicing the meat very thinly).

Ingredients:

2–4 lbs. of beef (inexpensive cuts), sliced thinly (venison and wild boar meat are very good for *tapa*)
Worcestershire sauce or plain vinegar
Salt and pepper to taste
2–3 bay leaves
3–4 cloves of garlic, crushed or diced

Mix enough Worcestershire sauce or vinegar to cover the thinly sliced beef (or other meat) with the rest of the ingredients. Marinate the slices in the refrigerator at least twelve hours or more. On a roasting rack over a pan of water, arrange the meat so it is spread without overlapping. Turn the oven to no more than 250 degrees so the meat dries slowly. It might take up to two hours. The fat drips into the water, preventing the process from being smoky. It tastes like American jerky.

"Swazi" Vegetable (from Josephine of Swaziland)

I do not know the Swazi name for this dish, but since it is something I learned to cook while in Swaziland, I have taken the liberty of calling it "Swazi vegetable." I hope my Swazi friends will understand.

Josephine was a distinguished-looking Swazi woman who was probably in her 40s. She came to the house five days a week to help with housekeeping chores, including cooking, cleaning the house, and doing the laundry. She told me once that I was not eating enough, that I looked a bit "skinny." In response, I kidded her that I certainly was not skinny, and that I thought I was quite muscular! She added that I should be plump and fat, and she was serious about it. "Thin as you are, Master," she continued, "the other Swazi maids probably think I am working for a poor man!"

I also recall when we were getting the house cleaned up and fixed for Judy's first visit to Swaziland, Josephine was making the twin beds in my bedroom. Then she spoke up. "Master, I think Mrs. Samonte will like it better if I put these two beds together." I thanked her, and told her to go ahead and take care of the details! That was Josephine, and she meant well. She was hard-working, kept the house clean and orderly, and made sure I was properly fed. She was worried about how I ate on weekends. I assured her that I would be all right on her days off.

Doing my own cooking one weekend led to a misadventure in my use of a pressure cooker. One Saturday afternoon I decided to prepare steamed rice and fried mongo beans to go with pork *adobo*. Dried mongo beans take at least an hour to cook unless they are soaked overnight. I was going to overcome this problem by cooking the mongo beans in the pressure cooker! I was aware that it is not advisable to use the pressure cooker for beans because it could clog up the pressure valve, and could lead to an exploded pot. I told myself that I would just have to check the valve regularly to avoid the problem. So, I embarked on this undertaking against the wise counsel of the designers of pressure cookers! When the cover to the valve started hissing and vibrating, I thought it was time to lift it a tiny bit, supposedly to decrease pressure build-up. Lo and behold, my mongo beans started coming out like a jet, out of the spout, and higher they went until they were plastered on the ceiling. It continued like a little Mount Vesuvius until the entire contents of the pressure cooker were stuck to the ceiling! It happened so fast I could not believe what was happening. I just moved back and watched helplessly.

As I looked at the kitchen ceiling newly decorated with boiled mongo, it suddenly occurred to me that Josephine must never find out about this. Thus, with a step ladder, one of my old towels and a bucket of water, I spent that Saturday afternoon scraping and wiping the ceiling, the kitchen floor and all the other surfaces where the spray had descended mercilessly. I must say the cleaning was accomplished without any trace of my clumsiness, and Josephine never found out that my intended dinner for that Saturday was plastered everywhere it was not supposed to be. Because of the time I spent cleaning up, I had to give up my plan to visit the Milwani Animal Park that afternoon for a photographic safari. As a consolation, I showered and treated myself that evening to a sumptuous dinner at one of my favorite restaurants in Swaziland.

Some weeks later, I was invited for dinner by one of my Swazi counterparts. I accepted gladly with one request. Could she include at least one typical Swazi dish? That would be no problem, she assured me. Among other things, she prepared a vegetable dish with a very nice nutty flavor. She explained how she flavored it with a small amount of freshly roasted and ground peanuts. To be sure that the dish was authentic, I later asked Josephine, who confirmed that it was indeed a local dish. I asked her to make it sometime. Sure enough, when she did, it was the same as the dish prepared for me when I was invited for dinner.

A couple of years later, when I had Swazi students at Eastern Michigan University, I included my version of the Swazi vegetable dish when I invited them for dinner at our house in Ann Arbor. The dish was passed around, and I watched their reactions closely. One looked at the dish for a while, took a small portion, tasted it, and quickly helped himself to a large portion. He looked at me and beamed. "Swazi," he acknowledged with an approving smile!

Ingredients:

1–2 bunches of greens roughly 2 inches in diameter if tied at the stems. (mustard, Swiss chard, collard green, beet greens, kale, turnip, even greens of carrots—Josephine retrieved the tops I had thrown away.)

1 medium tomato

1 medium onion

1 medium potato

1 teaspoon peanut butter

1 teaspoon cooking oil

Salt and pepper to taste

1 cup water

Dice the onion, tomato and potato. Sauté them together in one teaspoon of oil. Add salt and pepper to taste. Add chopped green vegetables and one cup of water. Simmer slowly for about 30 minutes, or until potato pieces are done and the greens tender. About five minutes before it is done, add one teaspoon of peanut butter. With potato masher, mix the ingredients in the pot (you can dispense with the mashing if you want to retain the shapes of the diced vegetables). Serve with rice and fried chicken or other roast meat.

Sinuman (from Lola Sabina)

Unlike *tupig*, which tended to be prepared mainly during the Christmas season in the Ilocos region, *sinuman* was made more frequently, especially when mangoes were plump and yellow. I have used substitutes in place of the milk from freshly grated coconuts and molasses from sugar cane.

Ingredients:

3 cups sweet rice, uncooked

3 1/2 cups water

1 (15 oz.) can cream of coconut (I like to use "Coco Lopez")

1 cup dark brown sugar

1 teaspoon anise seeds (more if you want)

Mix water and sweet rice in cooking pan as you cook rice. As soon as it boils, turn to low and cover. Cook about 30 minutes. While rice is cooking, pour can of coconut cream into a large frying pan. Add 1 cup of brown sugar and one teaspoon of anise seeds. Mix and let it simmer for about 10 minutes.

Empty cooked rice into the large frying pan with simmered coconut and sugar. Stir once in a while so each grain of rice is coated with the coconut mixture. Do not cover. Simmer for 20–30 minutes, carefully stirring occasionally.

Grilled Ampalaya Salad (from Lolo Colas)

Although busy with his law practice, business ventures, and daily trips to the farm, *Lolo* Nicolas sometimes contributed to the preparation of a dish for family meals. His selections were closer to the fare of peasants, quite different from those of *Lola* Leoncia, who was a graduate from a culinary school. I remember following him through a wooded area on our farm. He was looking for a particular plant that grew in the wild. He found it, and it was nothing more than a three-foot tall plant. I do not remember if it was a shrub or a vine. He seemed very pleased, and he asked Cadio to start digging. Cadio dug around the plant, which was not too difficult since the soil was sandy. After digging down about two feet, *Lolo* exclaimed "There it is!" It was a tuberous root probably three inches around and twenty inches long. "That," he said "is *pannarien.*" I did not know what it was for, but *Lolo* Nicolas seemed very pleased. We took the *pannarien* home that evening.

Lolo Nicolas showed the houseboy how to grate the *pannarien* after it was properly washed and peeled. The grated root was soaked in water for a few days. The grated white substance had the consistency and color of *yucca* or *cassava* root and was later squeezed into a bowl. This yielded a milky liquid. For breakfast, along with *estrellado* (fried egg) and some *pandesal* (crusty roll), *Lolo* Nicolas fried some rice left over from the previous night. As he fried the rice, he poured a little bit of the *pannarien* juice into the rice. Surprise! The rice changed into something like gelatinous rice (sweet rice) with a nutty flavor. We had breakfast together, and he must have been amused to see me finish that fried rice with *pannarien* in no time flat!

The recipe included here is for his grilled *ampalaya* salad. The procedure was the same when he also grilled some semi-hot peppers that were elongated and thin like fingers.

Ingredients:

1 dozen small *ampalaya* (bitter melon) — each about the size of an apricot (it is slightly more bitter than the long and larger variety usually sold at Chinese grocery stores)
1 medium tomato
1/8 small onion (or 4 green onions)
1/2 teaspoon amount of fresh ginger, diced
Bagoong or *patis* to taste (for Ilocanos mainly)
A little hot pepper (*sili ti sairo*) (this is optional)
Calamansi or lemon juice (optional)

Grill the *ampalaya* on charcoal or under the broiler. It should be grilled sufficiently to have some burned spots. Cut grilled *ampalaya*, scrape seeds out, slice flesh and set aside. Dice tomato, onion and ginger and mix with sliced *ampalaya*. Add *bagoong* or *patis* to taste. Add sliced hot pepper and onion if you wish. This makes a good side dish to accompany greasy meat dishes. But one needs to develop a taste for *ampalaya*. Remember, in some villages in Ilocos Norte, *ampalaya* juice is still applied to the nipple of a nursing mother when it is time to wean the baby.

Chicken Adobo (from Roly)

Whenever I have visited the Philippines since the 1960s, my brother, Roly, has surprised me with his cooking. It is a skill that I never associated with him for his profession as a mining engineer involved a lot of field trips to remote places in the Philippines, activities I did not associate with learning how to cook exotic dishes. But whenever there were family parties, he volunteered to prepare a dish, sometimes *paella*, *caldereta* (goat stew), or *sukiyaki*. For this book, I decided to include his version of chicken *adobo*, another family favorite that many Americans have readily learned to like.

Ingredients:

6–10 chicken thighs (or any part you prefer, or mixed parts)—can use pork instead of chicken
3–4 cloves of garlic (crushed)
2–3 bay leaves
black pepper, freshly ground
1/3 or more cup soy sauce
1/3 or more cup vinegar

Mix garlic, bay leaves, pepper, soy sauce and vinegar to marinate chicken, refrigerated, for 2–3 hours. You do not have to marinate the chicken if you do not have time, but marinating it allows the flavor to saturate the chicken (and/or pork).

Place the whole mixture in a frying pan. Include the marinade after meat has been marinated. Simmer covered for about 30 minutes to tenderize the chicken. Simmer for additional 20–30 minutes, uncovered, until the liquid is completely reduced. There is enough liquid from the chicken, vinegar and soy sauce to cook the chicken if allowed to simmer only. If liquid dries up before chicken is cooked (because the heat was set too high), add 1/3 to 1/2 of a cup of water. When liquid is completely reduced from 45 minutes to an hour, attend to it. Allow it to brown, turning as needed so as not to burn it. The browning brings out that special flavor that only *adobo* can give!

The same procedure and ingredients can be used in cooking pork *adobo*, but requires two cups of water to tenderize the pork. You can use country spare ribs, but you have to cook it longer than chicken. You can also combine chicken and pork when cooking *adobo*, but cook the pork 30 minutes before adding the chicken.

Spaghetti With Clam Sauce (from a small London restaurant)

When Judy and I were exploring some of the little streets surrounding Piccadilly Circus in London many years ago, we came upon a small Italian restaurant. I believe its name was *Il Cucciolo*. We went inside and we were pleasantly surprised to find a small, neat and tastefully decorated restaurant. White table cloths and cloth napkins dressed the wood tables. We enjoyed a few Italian dishes there whenever we visited London. One of my favorite appetizers was a small dish of *spaghetti a la vongole*. The waiter was kind enough to share the recipe. My attempts to reproduce it at home have not been too bad. I have included it here as a salute to that delightful Italian restaurant for it has given Judy and me much pleasure and many pleasant memories.

Ingredients:

1 medium onion, diced
1 medium to large tomato, diced
1 or 2 (6 oz.) can(s) of minced clam
1 bay leaf
1 clove garlic (optional)
Salt and pepper to taste
1 tablespoon olive oil
Thin spaghetti (measure bundle with tip of index finger touching tip of thumb)
Garlic or onion powder

Put olive oil in the pan. Sauté diced onions and diced tomatoes. Add bay leaf. When onion turns translucent, add 1 or 2 cans of minced clam. Simmer and reduce a little. Meanwhile, put spaghetti in pot with boiling water and cook as directed. Drain cooked spaghetti and put a teaspoon of olive oil or butter in the empty pot in which the spaghetti was boiled and sauté a little onion or garlic powder until it changes color slightly. Put back drained spaghetti in its cooking pot and mix it with the garlic or onion flavored olive oil. Place spaghetti on a dish, and pour the reduced clam sauce on top. Serve with green salad, crusty bread, and a glass of wine. This dish can be prepared within 20 minutes.

Roasted Peanuts (from Baket Uding)

Why devote space to the common peanut? For me, the *inurno nga mani* (roasted peanuts) evokes memories of *Baket* Uding, the wrinkled and toothless vendor who set up her little table in front of the Cine Reyes in Laoag. There was an assortment of snacks on her table that could be purchased for one *centavo*, such as two boiled bananas (*linengta nga dip-pig*), boiled or roasted corn (*mais*) on the cob, boiled *camote* (*camotig*), pickled (*inartem*) *santol, carmay*, or green papaya, which were bottled in murky looking fluid, and boiled or roasted peanuts in their shells.

There were other vendors like *Baket* Uding located in front of the local movie house. There were two small carts that were pushed right in front of the building every afternoon. They only sold *halo halo* (fresh and candied fruits mixed with evaporated milk and crushed ice). There was another table with about half a dozen bottles of *basi* (sugar cane wine), three or four small glasses, and a pail of water in which the glasses were dunked briefly after each customer. It cost two *centavos* for a glass of *basi*. There was also the woman who usually brought a basin-full of *pancit* (fried noodles with chicken and/or pork). She would situate herself near one of the regular vendors. Her *pancit* was a popular item, even if it was a nickel for each little bowl. But the *pancit* vendor also had competition. A woman with a *banga*, a large black earthen pot, filled with steaming *pinapaitan* (beef kidney, liver, tripe etc., heavily spiced and flavored with bile to give it a slightly bitter taste, and boiled) showed up at about the time the movie started in mid-afternoon. She also charged five *centavos* for a small bowl of *pinapaitan*.

At another stand was *Nana* Ay-yang who sold the same items as *Baket* Uding, along with the usual cigarettes with brand names like Chesterfield, Piedmont, Lucky Strike and Kool. These were sold by the pack or by individual cigarettes. *Nana* Ay-yang had one advantage over *Baket* Uding. *Nana* Ay-yang had popular magazines like *Banawag* in Ilocano, *Liwayway* in Tagalog, and some comic books which she rented to the kids at one *centavo* per reading, but only to the ones who paid!

This is where I came in as a participant to the free enterprise system that sprouted in front of Cine Reyes. Mother and Father bought me comic books like *Action*, *Batman and Robin*, *The Submariner*, *Flash*, *The Human Torch*, etc. When I was done with them, I took them to *Nana* Ay-yang and she rented them until they were sold. Since Cine Reyes was next door to the Segundo house, I visited *Nana* Ay-yang's table two or three times a day to check if my comic books were already sold. It got to a point when she would inform me right away when she saw me that they were not sold yet. Meanwhile I could see that her rental business was thriving! Eventually my used comic books would be sold, and that is how I got my allowance from my parents. I got my comic books and my allowance in the process. Incidentally, I should note that the comic book was a strong incentive for me when I was learning how to read. From comic books, I finally progressed to the *Readers' Digest* which, I understand, was written for high school level reading.

People who went to the movies bought some of the vendors' selections, and you can imagine the litter on the floor of the movie house. Every morning kids would be hired to sweep the floor in exchange for free admission in the evening.

Even more important in my recollection of the roasted peanuts that we bought from *Baket* Uding were the afternoons Father and I spent together on the porch. I was still of preschool age, and together, we shelled peanuts and enjoyed them while they were still warm. We did not talk much but it was comforting to be with Father, especially after he had spent most of the day at work. It was a nice break from playing all day with my friends in the neighborhood.

Incidentally, when I was in grade school, it was to vendors like *Baket* Uding that I sold outdated newspapers, which she then used for wrapping peanuts or pickles. Including my recipe for roasting peanuts in their shell was prompted by my experiences with those I bought from grocery stores in the U.S. which were sometimes overdone and consequently tasted slightly bitter. Hence, here is my recipe for roasting peanuts; I am quite pleased with the result.

I buy raw peanuts in the shell. Set the oven at 350 F, lay the unshelled peanuts on a pie tin, arranged in a single layer and roast for no more than 16 minutes (allowing for variations between ovens). Take them out of the oven immediately, and enjoy peanuts roasted as they should be, reminiscent of *Baket* Uding's if I may say so.

Glossary

Terms And Acronyms

Except for the words that are obviously of Spanish or English derivation, most of the terms listed below are Ilocano as used in the province of Ilocos Norte.

abal-abal — A June bug-like insect that comes out in profusion before the rainy season in the Ilocos region.

adobo — Chicken and/or pork simmered in a marinade to tenderize and later browned. It is spiced and marinated for an hour or two in a mixture of bay leaves, ground pepper, garlic, and vinegar.

aloti-it — house lizard.

Aglipayan religion — An indigenous Philippine Protestant movement named after its first Supreme Bishop, Gregorio Aglipay, a former member of the Roman Catholic clergy.

ampalaya or **paria** — bitter melon.

anangka — can weigh as much as 50 kilos, considered largest edible fruit.

angelus — church bell rung as a call for devotional prayers.

arroz caldo — thick soupy rice and chicken.

asotea — an extension of the kitchen and/or dining area without a roof, sometimes called *bansag* in small houses.

aswang — half-human and half-animal inhabitant of the spirit world.

bagoong — fish preserved with a lot of salt similar to salted anchovies.

baket — old woman.

banga — clay pot for cooking.

barrio — a political sub-division of the *poblacion* or town.

basi — sugar cane wine.

bayog — species of bamboo with thick stem wall and small central hole.

beclat — python.

bibingka — cake made from gelatinous rice flour, coconut milk and sugar. Sometimes flour from cassava or yucca is used.

bwa — betel nut (areca nut) — an ingredient mixed with betel pepper leaves, lime, and tobacco, and used like chewing tobacco.

biscotso — hard and crusty biscuit.

bolo or boneng — knife with a large blade used mainly as a tool by the Ilocano farmers, used also as a weapon during World War II by the *Bolo* Men.

botica — drug store.

Caballero — honorary title given to citizen for service to the Spanish Colonial government.

Cabeza de Barangay — chief of a district or section of a town.

cadena de amor — vine with little pink flowers shaped like a heart.

caimito — sometimes known as "star apple" because of its star pattern when cut in half cross-wise.

caldereta — goat stew.

calesa — two wheeled passenger cart drawn by a horse

capre — "black" and malevolent spirit that inhabits trees, especially the acacia trees.

carabasa — squash.

caratela — two wheeled utility cart drawn by a horse.

chocolate eh — "eh" is a code word (for **espeso**) between the priest and his houseboy to prepare a cup of good thick chocolate for an honored guest as opposed to chocolate "ah" (for **aguado**), a watered down version for less important visitors (from Jose Rizal's *Noli Me Tangere*).

cotsay — chives.

dinardaraan — pork cooked in pork blood with spices.

dinubla — tobacco rolled in tobacco leaves like a cigar, a favorite in the villages.

DODDS — Department of Defense Dependents School.

EMU — Eastern Michigan University.

farmacia — drug store.

FEATI — Far Eastern Air Transportation Inc.

gallera — roofed enclosure where roosters are brought to compete in cock fights for betting.

gamosa — suede.

gawed — betel pepper leaves for chewing with betel nut.

gosgosilat — a small shrub with strong y-shaped branches used for slingshot, its milky substance when a branch is broken is used as antiseptic, sometimes called "bolbolding" in other parts of the Ilocos region.

guerrilleros — insurgents who fight and run to harass their enemy. In the Philippines they fought the Japanese soldiers.

igad — gadget for grating coconut.

ina mother.

kilawen — generic term for seafood or meat dish eaten raw or slightly cooked with spices.

La Vanguardia — Spanish newspaper published at one time in the Philippines.

ladek — residue from reduced coconut cream.

lakay — old man.

lavandera — laundry woman.

lola — grandmother.

lolo — grandfather.

lomo — pork or beef loin.

longanisa — sausage.

maestra — teacher.

malabi — clay pot for household storage of water.

Mama Ti — a special term for Auntie Cristina, Father's eldest sister.

manong — term of respect for older male.

mangmangkik — an invisible and mischievous spirit that lurks in the woods.

mongo or **balatong** — tiny green dry beans.

MTC — Mobile Teacher Center.

paella — Chicken and rice dish with other ingredients including ham, chorizo and seafood cooked with olive oil, saffron, garlic, pimento, onions and tomato. (same as arroz valenciana).

PAL— Philippine Air Lines.

panaderia — bakery.

pannarien — tuber harvested from the woods processed and used to thicken rice or other dishes.

pancit — noodle dish.

pandesal — crusty breakfast roll.

pandesito — soft breakfast roll.

patis — fish sauce that separates from preserved salted fish.

pinakbet — vegetable stew with eggplant as principal ingredient.

pinapaitan — made from inexpensive cuts of beef, liver, kidney, tripe, etc. heavily spiced and also flavored with bile, and boiled. When made of goat meat, it is usually dry and served as *kilawen* (slightly grilled).

pulutan — a snack, usually of meat or seafood, eaten especially when drinking some alcoholic beverage.

PVTA— Philippine Virgina Tobacco Administration.

rosal — gardenia, usually with multiple petals, white and fragrant.

sarabo — gift.

saraguelas — also known as Jamaica plum or Spanish plum, sometimes yellow or purple.

sinuman — gelatinous rice cooked with coconut cream and molasses or sugar.

sinan padi — "like a priest," an inhabitant of the spirit world.

sinan castila — "like a Spaniard".

Tabacalera — Spanish corporation that dealt with production and sale of tobacco.

taga daya — "from the east."

taga laod — "from the west."

tapa — preserved meat salted, spiced and dried in the sun, similar to jerky.

tia — aunt.

tio — uncle.

Tio Papa — special name nephews and nieces gave to Uncle Damaso, Father's brother.

tupig — a sweet made of gelatinous flour with coconut cream and sugar, wrapped in banana leaves and roasted over charcoal, usually prepared during Christmas season in the Ilocos Region.

tuyo — sun-dried fish.

UM — University of Michigan.

UP — University of the Philippines, elsewhere in the book UP is also used to refer to the Upper Peninsula of Michigan.

USAID — United States Agency for International Development.

Sources

Books and Documents

Adams, Don, et al. (1983). Report of the Second External Evaluation Team, North Yemen Project.

Agas, Gloria L. Selected Herbal Plants: Uses by Selected Residents of Tagudin, Ilocos Sur, Philippines. (Unpublished Manuscript.)

Al-Khader. (1985). Letter of Dr. M. Al-Khader, Dean of the College of Education, University of Sanaa, Yemen. It documents his evaluation of the USAID/EMU project during the tenure of the author as "Chief of Party" of the Yemen Project.

Ansary, Tanim. (2002).West of Kabul, East of New York, Farrar, Straus and Giroux, New York.

Carson, Rachel. (1962) Silent Spring, Fawcett Publications, Inc.

Chodes, John. (2002) A Howling Wilderness. (A play about the trial of American military officers accused of mass killings of Filipinos during the Filipino-American war, reviewed in *Filipinas*.)

Custodio, Teresa, Project Director. (1998). Kasaysayan, The Story of the Filipino People, Asia Publishing Company Limited (10 volumes.)

Corpuz, O.D. (1965). The Philippines, Prentice Hall, Inc.

Corpuz, O.D. (1997). (1997). An Economic History of the Philippines, University of the Philippines Press.

Coseteng, Alicia M. L. (1972). Spanish Churches of the Philippines. New Mercury Printing Press, Quezon City.

Fernandez, Doreen G. (1994). TIKIM, Essays on Philippine Food and Culture, Anvil Publishing Inc., Philippines.

Fernandez, Alicia M. L. (1997). Fruits of the Philippines, Bookmark Inc., Philippines.

Griggers, Camilla Benoliar & Lluch, Sari Raissa. (2002). Film Producers, "Memories of a Forgotten War: A Documentary on the Philippine-American War of 1899." (Premiered at the University of the Philippines, January, 2002.)

Hara, Captain Teimichi. (1962). Japanese Destroyer Captain, Ballantine Books.

Jose, R. Regalado. (1999). A Chronology of Ilocos Norte History.

Jose, F. Sionil. (1998). Dusk, The Modern Library.

Krumm, Bob (1996). The Great Lakes Berry Book, Falcon, Helena, Montana.

Philippine Overseas Employment Administration. Source for data on Filipinos employed overseas.

Roces, Alfredo, Editor. (1978). Filipino Heritage, The Making of a Nation, (10 volumes), Lahing Pilipino Publishing, Inc.

Samonte, Carol S. (2003). Unpublished manuscript about the arrival of one group of guerrillas in the town of Solsona, Ilocos Norte.

Samonte, Damaso T. Memoirs, Unpublished Manuscript.

Samonte, Judith. (2002). Paintings of the Samonte and Segundo ancestral homes were based on old photographs. Other illustrations by Judy were based on her first hand visits to the Philippines, consultations with me, with relatives and with Filipino friends.

Samonte, Richard (2002). Unpublished article about the Samonte family in Chicago.

Segundo, Alicia D. (October 16, 2002). Letter about how she remembered Mother's thoughtfulness and resourcefulness.

Smith, Steven Trent. (2001).The Rescue, 40 Americans Trapped in the Philippines. A Set of Secret Japanese Battle Plans. And the Submarine That Saved Them., John Wilen & Sons, Inc.

Takaki, Ronald. (revised, 1998). Strangers from a Different Shore, Little, Brown and Company.

The Ann Arbor News, January 10, 2002; February 19, 2002; November 16, 2003.

The Mining Journal, Marquette, August 22, 2002.

TIME, January 21, 2002; November 3, 2003.

Traver, Robert. (2001). *Traver on Fishing*, Edited with an introduction by Nick Lyons, The Lyons Press, Guildford, Connecticut.

World Bank Document. Source for data on poverty in the Philippines.

Conversations

The surviving siblings of Mother — *Tio* Salio, *Tio* Gli and Auntie Angeles — provided information about the Segundo family. Auntie Angeles recalled, in connection with *Lola* Leoncia's political activities and leadership in the Philippine Women's Club on the provincial level, some of the visitors to the Segundo house. They included Elpidio Quirino and Diosdado Macapagal, long before either became president of the Philippines. She also mentioned the three-day stay at the Segundo house of three national leaders of the Philippine Women's club. *Tio* Salio recalled some of the business ventures of *Lolo* Nicolas while *Lolo* was still a college student in Manila, including *Lolo* Nicolas' recollection of being at the Luneta when Jose Rizal was executed by the Spaniards. *Tio* Gli talked about his experience when he was incarcerated with *Tio* Deriong by the Japanese Military Police in the town of Laoag.

Cousin Ruth Samonte-Limjuco, daughter of Damaso Samonte and Pacita Dancel, augmented the information about the Samonte family in the Philippines, and also added to my recollections about our own childhood. Some of her accounts about her visits with Father and Mother when I was already in the United States were also useful.

Cousin Helen Samonte-Shippy, daughter of Damaso Samonte and Pacita Dancel, supplemented and verified some of my recollections about *Mama* Ti, *Tio Papa* and *Lola* Sabina. Since she represents a younger group of cousins than my own (e.g., Erning, Romeo, Sigrid, Ruth, Evelyn, and Josephine), her observations provided additional perspectives about the Samonte family.

Cousin Anita Samonte-Jencks, daughter of Fortunato Samonte and Venancia Siazon, clarified some of the information about the early years of the Samonte brothers in Chicago. She elaborated on some of the materials I recalled from conversations I had with Uncle Fort, Aunt Ven, and Uncle Larry whenever I visited Chicago for vacation.

Extended conversations with my brother, Carol ("Roly") Samonte, focused on Father's and my brother's trip from Manila to Laoag just after the Japanese invasion of the Philippines in December, 1941. It was a trip that ordinarily took about 10–12 hours by bus, but it took Father and Roly five days traveling during the day and using means of transportation other than motorized vehicle. Roly has also been very helpful in clarifying some aspects of our complicated family tree, and in recalling the ingredients of a few of the recipes included in this book. His unpublished manuscript on the war years in Solsona provided some interesting materials for Father's role as commander of the *Bolo* Battalion in Solsona.

My sister, Astrid Samonte Gorospe, added information about Father and Mother, especially dealing with the period when I was already in the United States. She diligently collected census data and maps of Laoag. She also duplicated some of the chapters that were e-mailed to her so that they could be shared with other relatives for review.

Consultations with *Tio* Salio by my sister, Amy Samonte-Benavides, supplemented the information I collected from my own interview of *Tio* Salio.

Conversations with a number of relatives from Marquette were very useful when I wrote "To Da Woods." Their reactions to my account of Michigan's Upper Peninsula added more clarity to my perceptions of some of the sub-cultures in Marquette and vicinity. These relatives include Gene and Jean Elzinga, and Don and Kay Elzinga. Gene and Don are Judy's brothers.

Deling Agas Weller, Lecturer in Language and Culture, University of Michigan, and her sister, Gloria Lorenzana Agas, have been valuable sources on medicinal plants in the Philippines. Deling and Gloria have also been very helpful whenever I called them to refresh my memory about some obscure Ilocano word or expression.

Joanne Tangorra, a professional editor and a university instructor in English composition, has been very encouraging after reading portions of the manuscript.

Our good neighbors at Lakeshore Boulevard in Marquette, Robert and Joan Rafferty, long-time residents of the Upper Peninsula, were helpful with their reactions and comments after reading a draft of the book. Bob, who retired from the Department of Natural Resources of Michigan, has been instrumental in suggesting the use of maps to facilitate the placement of towns, buildings in Laoag, river, etc. mentioned in the book.

Author and Illustrator

Photo by: Christine Garceau Photography, Marquette, MI.

Quirico S. Samonte, Jr., Ph.D. Professor Emeritus, Eastern Michigan University, is a graduate of the University of the Philippines and of the University of Michigan. He served as Exchange Professor in England (1968–1969), Advisor to the Kingdom of Swaziland (1979–1981) under a USAID/EMU project, and as "Chief of Party" in North Yemen (1984-1985) under a USAID/EMU project. He was awarded "Outstanding Filipino Overseas" by the Philippine government in 1982, and was given a "Lifetime Distinguished Professional Achievement Award" by the University of the Philippines Alumni Association of America in 1999.

Judith E. Samonte, M.A. Research Associate (retired) of the Institute for Social Research, University of Michigan. She earned her undergraduate degree in Anthropology and her graduate degree in Sociology from the University of Michigan. She drew the Illustrations for this book.